Metatron

About the Author

Spiritualist minister Rose Vanden Eynden earned her mediumship certification from the Indiana Association of Spiritualists in 2000. She is a founding member of the United Spiritualists of the Christ Light (USCL) Church in Cincinnati, Ohio, where she serves as a minister and instructor. She conducts personal readings and workshops across the country. Her book *So You Want to Be a Medium? A Down-to-Earth Guide* has been translated into two languages, and her work has been featured in national magazines, regional newspapers, and on radio and television.

Metatron

Invoking the Angel of God's Presence

Rose Vanden Eynden

Llewellyn Publications
Woodbury, Minnesota

First Edition
Third Printing, 2009

Cover design by Kevin R. Brown
Cover illustration © Koralik Associates / Eric Williams
Interior book design by Joanna Willis
Interior illustrations by Llewellyn art department

Llewellyn is a registered trademark of Llewellyn Worldwide, Ltd.

Library of Congress Cataloging-in-Publication Data
Vanden Eynden, Rose.
   Metatron : invoking the angel of God's presence / by Rose Vanden
Eynden. — 1st ed.
      p. cm.
   Includes bibliographical references and index.
   ISBN 978-0-7387-1343-4
   1. God—Miscellanea. 2. Spiritual life—Miscellanea. 3. Angels—
Miscellanea. 4. Occultism. I. Title.
   BF1999.V34 2008
   202'.15—dc22
                                                      2008014716

Llewellyn Publications
A Division of Llewellyn Worldwide, Ltd.
2143 Wooddale Drive, Dept. 978-0-7387-1343-4
Woodbury, MN 55125-2989, U.S.A.
www.llewellyn.com

Printed in the United States of America

This book is dedicated to my father,
William C. Finley,
who taught me many things about discipline
and faith, even if he isn't so sure about angels.
I love you, Daddy. I'll believe for both of us.

Contents

$\mathscr{A}$cknowledgements

The following people submitted questions for the Archangel Metatron to answer in this book, and I want to thank them for their contributions: Shey Barnwell, Brenda Carpenter, Thembi Carr, Mary Lynn Crawford, Carol Dell'Alba, Liss Dickerson, Angie Fellner, Shelley Goldman, Tammy Hodge, Lori Leach, Cindy Mullen, Ron Muskopt, Shannon Muskopt, Irene Olivier, Kandy Riley, Robert Rivard, Rev. Christine Sabick, Suzanne Segrati, Amber Siewertsen, Linda Simonsen, Cathy Switzer, Heather Thomas, Keith Vanden Eynden, Shellie Warren, Tomi Weimer, and Michelle Wisbith.

Introduction

Angels have been around me since I was a child.

I don't mean that literally. Throughout my Roman Catholic upbringing, angels were a part of my religious instruction and tradition. I attended Saint Michael the Archangel parish and school, for goodness' sake. From first grade through high school, I was taught that angels were watching over me. Every time I attended Mass, I passed a statue of Archangel Michael, standing tall and righteous with armor and sword, his heel resting on the head of the serpent, the Devil in disguise. I listened to the stories from the Bible: Archangel Gabriel's announcement of Mary's immaculate pregnancy, the dazzling appearance of angels proclaiming Jesus's birth and their pronouncement of Jesus's resurrection at his tomb, the war described in the Book of Revelation between the angels and the forces of evil. Angels were referred to in the prayers recited and the songs sung at services. I never disputed their existence, but I certainly didn't believe they affected me in the least.

Perhaps, like me, you grew up with angels on the periphery of your world. Angel stories are not exclusive to Christianity; they permeate many cultures and religious traditions. They are not confined to any one location on the planet or any single spiritual path. Islam holds that its holy book, the Quran, was dictated to the prophet Muhammad by the Archangel Gabriel. The Mormon religion was given to its founder, Joseph Smith, by an angel named Moroni. The wings and influence of angels seem to stretch in many directions, lovingly overshadowing humanity in peace, compassion, and higher knowledge. Even a quick perusal of the Internet today reveals thousands of accounts of personal encounters with angelic beings. These bloggers and discussion group members come from all walks of life, from diverse cultures, backgrounds, and religious traditions. How is it that angels can influence so many different people in such remarkable ways?

Angels are not human, nor do they act with human habits. We tend to give them human characteristics as a way of classifying and understanding them. By nature, we try to sort our experiences into tidy little boxes. Just look at the depictions of angels in popular culture. The blockbuster film *City of Angels* told the story of an angel who, after falling in love with a human woman, chose to undergo a transformation to become a man. In the TV series *Touched by an Angel,* Monica, the angelic caseworker learning how to help her earthly charges, has a very human weakness for mocha lattes. Even Clarence, the angel-second-class in the Christmas favorite *It's a Wonderful Life,* carries around his favorite novel, *Tom Sawyer.* Althought these attributes might be endearing to the human audiences watching these characters, real angels do not fall in love, drink coffee, or read Mark Twain (or any other author) for pleasure.

But although we insist on humanizing angels, they were created by God as entities completely separate from human beings. This is why angels can be in so many different places at once, serving a variety of needs and desires. They are not limited by a body, as we are, and they understand Natural Law, the axioms that govern God's Universe, in ways that we don't—which allows them to perform what we see as miraculous interventions. Such situations, where angels appear and save people from certain injury or death, can be mind-boggling to us. For angels, there is no miracle involved. It's just what they do.

Whether serving humanity on a large scale or attending to one person, angels act always in the highest, most Divine love energy. Small tasks are as important to them as large ones; one person matters just as much as the population of an entire country. Perhaps this is why belief in angels is so prevalent in society today. In a 2004 Gallup poll, 78 percent of Americans indicated a belief in angels.[1] At our core, we recognize our spiritual connection to Creator, and we believe that His servants, the angels, won't desert us—but the belief is a dormant, inactive one.

I suppose I fell into this category at one time, too. Given the angel stories and invocations of my upbringing, that

---

1 Cited in "Angels in Christianity," www.religionfacts.com/ christianity/beliefs/angels.htm, accessed April 7, 2008.

belief always dwelled in the back of my mind, but I had no reason to believe angels were really and tangibly involved in my life. Not until a few years ago, anyway.

It was one of those days. We all have them—days when we feel emotionally spent, frustrated with everything, and ready to jump the next jet to the Bahamas. I was at home. It was my day off, but I hadn't accomplished anything I'd intended. I'd spent hours racking my brain about my next writing project. Should I return to my novel, which was languishing on my hard drive, or start something completely different? The notion of a new project appealed to me, but I had no idea what to write about. I toyed with a couple of concepts, but neither grabbed me with the force of inspiration that had come to me with my first nonfiction book. After staring at a blank computer screen for several hours, I was convinced I'd never figure out what I was supposed to do, and I would certainly never be published again. (Yeah, we all have our negative moments. I'm no exception—and I can be overly dramatic. Did I mention I majored in theatre in college?)

Wallowing in self-doubt, I decided to meditate, hoping to find some clarity about my purpose in life. I should point out that I've been meditating for years. I teach mediumship classes, and meditation is one of the most important tools I teach my students. It is a gateway to the other side, to worlds that would amaze so many people if they just learned the process. I've had many exciting and wondrous experiences during meditation. I've had an equal number of dull and uninspiring sessions, too, when my brain just doesn't want to engage.

On the afternoon in question, my meditation was going the unproductive route. (Big surprise, right?) I was just ready to quit and chalk up another failed session when, in my mind, I suddenly saw a flash of brilliant white light. I found myself looking up into a blinding cone of flame that stretched up as far as I could see: a lightning bolt of continuous energy, blazing before me. I was overcome with a warm, intense feeling of strength and compassion. As I sat spellbound with awe, a name rocketed through my mind.

Metatron.

It resounded in my head with such force I was shaken immediately out of my meditative state. My eyes flew open, and I looked around the familiar surroundings of my bedroom, my favorite place to meditate. Everything looked the same, but I felt completely different. My heart raced with excitement because I knew now what my next writing project would be. I had found my purpose.

Metatron.

If the name isn't ringing a bell for you, you're not alone. Not many people recognize it. At the time, it was vaguely familiar to me, but I couldn't quite put my finger on why. Still, I was excited. I had been given a message in my meditation, and, being a good medium and follower of Spiritualist teachings, I was going to tenaciously examine it until I understood every aspect of it.

Movie fans may recognize the name Metatron from the film *Dogma*. As people close to me know, I am a true child of popular culture and have a great love for film as well as theatre. At the point in my life when I considered becoming a journalist, my fondest dream was to be a film critic.

Film has always moved me, and a good movie resonates in my mind and heart long after the final scene fades. *Dogma* was one of those movies for me.

Written and directed by Kevin Smith, *Dogma* was released in 1999 to critical acclaim and religious outrage. The story of two banished angels who find a loophole in Catholic Church doctrine—a loophole that will let them return to heaven and thus, unfortunately, erase all of existence—ignited protests from religious institutions because of its subject matter; its obscene language and references to drinking, drug use, and sexuality; its violence; and its depiction of God Himself (or, more accurately in this case, God Herself). I followed the controversy with great interest, although I didn't see the film myself until it was released on video a year or so later. My reaction to the movie? I loved it. I tend to find religious humor hysterical, which probably stems from my Catholic upbringing. After all, if we can't poke fun at our belief systems, what can we laugh about? A pointed look at religious doctrines and their effects on us as human beings, *Dogma* remains a funny and smart, albeit crude, satire of Christian theology.

But the thing that stuck with me about *Dogma* wasn't the script's acerbic wit (which it has) or any particularly great performances (although several of the actors are quite good). It was a particular scene near the beginning of the film, where the protagonist, Bethany, is awakened in her bedroom by a flash of fire and a booming voice proclaiming, *"Behold the Metatron, herald of the Almighty and voice of the one true God."* The fire burns as the voice intones this ominous greeting—until Bethany douses the flames with a fire extinguisher and the voice starts coughing and sputtering. When the haze of smoke and chemicals clears, Bethany sees a man standing there—well, at least she thinks it's a man until a huge pair of wings sprouts from his back.

This winged creature introduces himself as the Metatron, also known as the Voice of God, the messenger who speaks to human beings whenever the Creator has some wisdom to impart or some task to assign. He also explains that he is a Seraph, one of the angels of the highest order, the Seraphim who sit closest to God's throne.

The introduction of this angel in the movie fascinated me. The idea that God Himself did not speak, but used an angelic instrument as His voice, intrigued me. I had never heard of Metatron. (I was playing my part: the character actually mentions that humanity is so grossly ignorant that it knows nothing of him.) The wheels in my head turned throughout the rest of the film as I waited for this character to reappear and to tell us more about himself.

But you know Hollywood. It's all about entertainment, flash, and fun. Although actor Alan Rickman made a sincerely sarcastic and wickedly funny Metatron, Kevin Smith wrote the character with humor, not accuracy, in mind. The role didn't do Metatron justice.

Finding more information on Metatron proved a daunting task. I soon realized that although he was mentioned in almost every text on angels I read, rarely was more than a paragraph or two devoted to him. Every source commented on him as a powerful entity, one very close to Creator. If

Metatron was so important, why, then, was so little known and recorded about him? This mystery, as well as the booming name still reverberating in my head, spurred me to continue my quest. This book grew from that research—and from Metatron's own challenge to me.

Metatron, the Archangel of the Presence, is as real and tangible as the chair you sit in as you read this. He is as close as the heart pumping blood within your chest and, if you choose, he can become as important to your everyday life as that very same circulatory system. If you are looking for a closer relationship with Creator, Metatron can facilitate it. He can, and will, become your closest angelic ally if you so desire it, and having an angel in your corner can benefit you in ways you may only think possible in dreams. Metatron can help with so many aspects of life, and he is only a petition away. This book will show you how to get in touch with Metatron in order to become a better you.

If you study and work with angels, you begin to understand that each has certain areas of expertise. Some of the better-known Archangels are called upon for their help in and affinity for particular situations. Perhaps you are familiar with the four main Archangels in Western thought and their traditional strengths. Let's review them here.

Archangel	Meaning of name	Main function	Patron of . . .	Invoke for . . .
Raphael	*Bright, shining healer*	To take care of sickness, disease, and imbalance in all God's creatures	Doctors, nurses, midwives, healers, travelers, the blind, children	Eliminating addictions, improving physical and spiritual sight, healing both humans and animals, retrieving lost pets, protection for travelers
Michael	*Who is God*	To lead the legions of angels; to defend the righteous and the weak	Police officers, military personnel, security guards, hunters, all sacred spaces and shrines	Strengthening commitment and dedication to beliefs; courage, energy, and vitality, finding life's purpose, motivation; protection; clearing space
Gabriel	*Governor of light*	To aid communication; convey messages from the spirit world; oversee birth and death, resurrection, transformation, mystery	Messengers, postal employees, journalists, writers, entertainers, all aspects of telecommunications	Reproductive and adoption issues, aiding communication in all forms
Uriel/Ariel	*Earth's great lord* or *God is Light*	To guard dreams, visions, prophecy; oversee all natural phenomena and the faerie kingdom; impart deep wisdom and knowledge	Lightworkers, animals, ecology, teachers, students	Responding to earthly changes such as weather and natural disasters, channeling Divine magick and spiritual understanding, aiding in studies and test-taking

Metatron is no different; he is fully as powerful and helpful as the four Archangels with whom most of us are familiar. Working with him can especially help you in these ways:

- balancing your masculine and feminine energies
- balancing your material and spiritual pursuits
- accessing the Akashic Records and balancing karmic issues (more on the Akashic Records later)
- bringing peace and understanding to your life issues related to past and current incarnations
- promoting better and more fulfilling relationships between you, others, and Creator

Like all angels, Metatron is personable, loving, and interested in benefiting humanity in any way possible. As I began to work with Metatron's energy, he impressed me with the following information, which I share with you with my own commentary:

- Metatron is available to work with anyone on any type of issue or problem. Nothing is too big or too small for his scope of practice. The only requirement is your sincere desire to better yourself and to bring love and blessings to those whose lives you touch. Like all angels, Metatron asks nothing in return for his help and guidance but your own devotion to promoting love—which is, ultimately, God—in the Universe. That's what angels are all about.

- Gratitude goes a long way in spiritual work. Don't forget to say thank you when something you have been asking for or working toward comes through for you. The angels, Metatron included, will gladly share their energy with you. That in itself is a humbling experience. Gratitude fosters the Divine connection we all have with our Creator and with all creations.

- Humility is a virtue that promotes spiritual growth. Have you heard the saying that EGO stands for "easing God out"? Working with angels can be an incredibly exciting adventure. Always remember, however, that angels work with *all* people who ask for their guidance and aid. They do not play favorites; they have no ego to speak of, so they never think about what benefit they themselves receive from the interaction. You are just as worthy of their attention as anyone else. The Serbians have a beautiful proverb: "Be humble, for you are made of earth. Be noble, for you are made of stars." Nowhere can this be felt more deeply than in spiritual pursuits and angelic communication.

- Angelic contact can be fun. Forging a relationship with Metatron, or any angelic entity, can be an intimidating prospect. Thoughts like *What if I'm doing it wrong?* or *I'm not worthy of this attention* do not serve you or anyone else on the planet. All angels, including Metatron, are forgiving and loving beings. They are chiefly concerned with humanity;

we are one of their most important charges. They realize we make mistakes, and they're OK with that. You must be OK with it, too. Remember to laugh. Angels have a high energy vibration, and laughter, which raises our own energy, helps us connect better with them. When you're feeling sad or upset, doesn't it usually help to watch a funny movie or recall a humorous story? Let yourself enjoy your angelic communications.

- It's wise to trust what you get from angelic contact. Because our society prizes scientific thought so highly, we have been trained from a very young age to favor the left side of our brain, the hemisphere that controls logical thinking. The right side, which controls creativity, imagination, and intuition, has been relegated to second-class status. The right brain, however, is the side we use to communicate with angels and Spirit. Because it's also the side in charge of imagination, we often think we are making up the images, words, or feelings we receive when we first open ourselves to angelic communion. *You are not making it up!* If you set your intention to work from a place of love when you ask Metatron, or any other angel, to be with you, then whatever you receive in your communications is truth. Trust it, and trust yourself!

Getting to know Metatron and learning to work with his energy are among the most rewarding things I've ever done. I have learned countless lessons about my own spiritual path that I'm not sure I would have discovered had he not led me to them. If you are ready to have a similar journey, I encourage you to keep reading, and to use this invocation to connect with Metatron.

An invocation is an appeal for help, usually of a spiritual nature. Just saying "Hey, Metatron, I could use some assistance," is actually an invocation, and you can always feel free to spontaneously call for his help if you need it, without worrying whether your words are perfect. But if you'd like something a little more formal, especially at the beginning, center yourself by taking a few slow, deep breaths, and then read these words aloud:

> *Archangel Metatron, wise counselor and genuine friend of*
> *   humanity,*
> *I speak to you now to forge a connection with you,*
> *A connection I hope to make stronger with each passing day.*
> *I hope to know you better.*
> *I hope to open my eyes, ears, and heart to your knowledge*
> *   and wisdom.*
> *I hope, with your help, to become the person I am meant to*
> *   be.*
> *Please know that it is my sincere desire to be of service to*
> *   God and humanity as I forge this connection,*
> *And help me to understand how I may best serve God's*
> *   plan.*
> *Thank you and bless you. And so it is, amen.*

What do you feel now that you've said this invocation? Try to notice everything, even little pricks or tingles in your body. Do you feel calm? Excited? Hot or cold? All of these can be messages to you, signals of Metatron's presence. You called him in, didn't you? He came, and these small signs let you know he's around. As you work with his energy, you may find that these signals intensify, proving that Metatron is right there with you when you need him. Pay attention to all the subtle thoughts and feelings that begin to emerge when you focus on connecting with Metatron. These are important and valid.

Now that you've been introduced to the Archangel, let's take some time to understand Metatron's background and history. When we meet a new friend, we often ask him where he's been, what he's been doing, and what his life's been like up to this point. That's a good place to start with Metatron, too.

ONE

*W*ho Is Metatron?

To better understand Metatron, it helps to first explore the general angelic kingdom. With a knowledge of the scope of these higher realms, you can see more clearly where Metatron fits into the grand scheme of things and why forging a relationship with him may benefit your spiritual growth. Angels are all around us and have been interacting with humanity ever since the Universe was created. Let's get to know more about them.

An Array of Angels

The angelic kingdom has three energetic *spheres,* but they need not be pictured as actual spheres. I like to think of them as concentric rings that revolve around Creator at the center, sort of like rings around the planet Saturn. And remember that the placement of the spheres does not imply order, intelligence, or rank in the sense of importance. All the angels, in whichever sphere they reside, are vital to God, just as we are all equally loved in Creator's eyes. Many angels, Metatron included, belong to several spheres, which indicates that the angels can move through these energy rings as the need arises.

Let's look for a moment at the angel hierarchy, as well as we can understand it from the human perspective. The hierarchy system most used by Western culture comes from a book written by Dionysius the Areopagite in the sixth century.[1] In imagining the spheres of angels as rings surrounding the "planet God," the First Sphere is closest to the center, with the Second Sphere outside of that, and the Third Sphere farthest from the middle—that is, closest to humanity. The classification *angels* is an umbrella term used to refer to any and all of these magnificent beings, no matter to which sphere they belong, even though the Third Sphere includes a specific group known as Angels.

In general, each of the spheres has an overarching function, and each group of angels within it concentrates its energies upon certain duties. For instance, the Angels of the First Sphere (the groups called the *Seraphim, Cherubim,* and *Thrones*) have the deepest knowledge of God and how Divinity manifests throughout the Universe. The Angels of the Second Sphere (comprised of the *Dominions, Powers,* and *Virtues*) are chiefly concerned with the cosmos and how it works, channeling energies that keep the Universe in constant movement and order. Finally, the Angels of the Third Sphere (the *Principalities, Archangels,* and *Angels*) are intricately involved with the matters of humanity. Within

---

1   Silver RavenWolf, *Angels: Companions in Magick* (St. Paul, MN: Llewellyn, 1996), 38.

these spheres, the angels also perform certain jobs pertaining to the groups to which they belong.

Angels of the First Sphere

Seraphim   Create positive energy, which carries through all realms

Cherubim   Offer Divine protection for all spiritual purposes

Thrones   Help smooth interactions between large groups of humans

Angels of the Second Sphere

Dominions   Integrate material and spiritual energies; oversee leadership roles and issues

Powers   Dispense justice in loving ways; record human history and oversee governments and religious institutions

Virtues   Move spiritual energy to human consciousness; serve as "miracle angels" and angels of nature

Angels of the Third Sphere

Principalities   Serve as guardians of large groups of people, such as countries; work toward reforms for humanity

Archangels   Work as mediators between Divinity and humanity

Angels   Are assigned to work with a particular person for matters of physical and Divine manifestation

The main purpose of angels is to promote the flow of Divine energy throughout all of creation. Remember that the earth is not the only project on God's plate. The Universe is vast, and what little we know about our solar system and its intricacies is just that—very little. Angels are messengers, helpers, channels, and they have many other positions within the Universe that we may never understand. We need to realize, however, that these powerful entities are made up of pure love and compassion. They intend to serve Creator in all things, and thus to further the agenda of love that God has for all of creation. Angels have no purpose higher than this; this is what they were created to do.

So now that we know a bit more about angels and their roles in the Universe, where does Metatron fit into this structure? It's quite fascinating, actually, so get comfortable in your chair and delve into the mystery with me!

The Angel of the Presence

Without question, Metatron is a powerful force. In the celestial hierarchy, he belongs to both the First and Third Spheres as a Seraph and an Archangel, which gives him a unique perspective and role. He dwells in the energy closest to the Divine and helps create positive love vibrations to sustain the Universe, but he is also chiefly concerned with humanity and its connection to that Divine force. This may be one of the reasons for his well-known nickname, the Angel of the Presence, and his role as the essential link between the human and the divine. The Hebrew term for this role, *Sar ha-Panim,* describes an angel that is a "visible manifestation of God."[2] Because of his close proximity to Creator and his intimate knowledge and love for humanity, Metatron is God's ultimate emissary.

The meaning of his name (sometimes spelled Metratton, Mittron, Metaraon, Merraton, and Matatron) is disputed; some believe it derives from the Latin word *metator,* meaning "to guide or measure," while others think it a Jewish invention.[3] I find it interesting to look at the Greek roots, too. The prefix "meta" means "to go beyond; to transcend." So the name could be a blend of the Greek-derived *meta* and *thronos,* meaning "beyond the throne," referring to Metatron's close proximity to Creator.[4] Both the Latin and Greek meanings seem to reflect Metatron's place in the angelic kingdom, and you'll see why as we continue to explore his history and lore.

Metatron is a prominent angelic figure in the Kabbalah, the prevalent system of Jewish mysticism. Here, Metatron governs the Tree of Life and its teachings, which embody the wisdom of the Kabbalah and the understanding of the Divine. Metatron resides in the place closest to God; he is sometimes depicted sitting on a throne next to God's, and some even call him "the lesser YHWH," or Yahweh (in Hebrew tradition, this is the ineffable name of God, the Tetragrammaton, which should not be spoken aloud). It is

---

2 Rabbi Geoffrey W. Dennis, *The Encyclopedia of Jewish Myth, Magic and Mysticism* (Woodbury, MN: Llewellyn, 2007), 56.

3 RavenWolf, *Angels,* 73.

4 Dennis, 170.

interesting to see Metatron being so closely linked to the Divine.

Metatron is also thought to be the supreme angel of death, handing out the orders from Creator to the angels Sammael and Gabriel, who carry out God's wishes. Some lore features him as the angel who led Abraham through Canaan and the children of Israel through the wilderness after Moses brought them out of Egypt. He is also thought to be the angel who wrestled Jacob in the desert, who prevented Abraham from sacrificing his son Isaac, and who revealed God's messages to Joshua.[5]

Another of his primary duties is to serve as chief scribe of the angelic realms. He is the keeper of the Akashic Records, the sacred tablets that chronicle every action and thought throughout the Universe. This job links him to the god Thoth of Egyptian lore, who is also associated with sacred geometry. Metatron has his own associations with this esoteric knowledge, as we'll see shortly.

But some stories refer to Metatron in ambiguous ways, with details that are hard to reconcile: for example, the idea that Metatron was once a human being named Enoch, who is mentioned in Genesis. This passage (Genesis 5:18–19 and 21–24) is from the *Good News Bible*:

> When Jared was 162, he had a son, Enoch, and then lived another 800 years . . . When Enoch was 65, he had a son, Methuselah. After that, Enoch lived in fellowship with God for 300 years and had other children. He lived to be 365 years old. He spent his life in fellowship with God, and then he disappeared, because God took him away.

---

5 Ibid.

According to the Book of Enoch, a noncanonical text not accepted in the body of recognized Biblical works, the man who was disappeared in Genesis was taken into heaven by God and transformed into the angel Metatron. When Enoch arrived in heaven, he was remade into a spirit of fire and given thirty-six pairs of wings and innumerable eyes. As a man, Enoch had been a prophet who tried to teach the people to obey God. Enoch invented books and writing and recorded the history of his people. The most important writings ascribed to him or his influence bear his name: the First, Second, and Third Books of Enoch. This third book, dating probably to the second century A.D., was dictated to the alleged author, Rabbi Ishmael, and details the rabbi's journey to heaven. This book's information on the angelic kingdom was imparted by the Archangel Metatron, who claimed to be the remade patriarch Enoch. This was Enoch's reward for his goodness on earth and for his talents as a scribe.

The parallels between the two are obvious, yet Metatron's previous identity as the man Enoch is a confusing concept. As we noted earlier, many esoteric thinkers believe angels to be separate entities from human beings, created by God for a specific purpose. The idea that humans die and become angels, although still prevalent in Western culture, is not accurate, according to most metaphysical schools of thought. According to Rabbi Geoffrey W. Dennis in his book *The Encyclopedia of Jewish Myth, Magic and Mysticism,* this "angelification" was used to depict the idea that a human being could become part of the divine assembly, thus experiencing *unio mystica,* or mystical union with

God.[6] Enoch seems to have been one of a handful of people to undergo this stunning transformation. This belief that Metatron was once a man makes his story unique in the lore surrounding the angelic kingdom and gives us even more insight into his nature and purpose.

The implication of Metatron's once-human nature is this: Metatron understands humanity, having lived as part of it. Metatron recognizes the challenges unique to the human experience, since he himself undertook many of them as the man Enoch. In many ways, Metatron takes on a Christ-like quality, for Jesus, too, sympathizes with human nature because of his own experience with it. Some esoteric thinkers believe that Christ is too busy and too evolved an entity to bother with enlightening those who seek the path to God. That being the case, these seekers may do well to enlist the aid of Metatron, whose own energy is very like the Christ's.

Is Christ too busy to bother with us mere mortals? I hardly think so. I believe that Metatron is interested in our welfare due to his angelic nature, the divine love that infuses his being and compels him to want to help us. Some of these mysterious forces will remain mysterious, but that doesn't mean that we can't seek the help of Christ or the guidance of Metatron if we need it. They are both great teachers who wish to impart their knowledge and wisdom to those who want it. And they are available at all times to every person. What a gift!

---

6 Ibid., 16.

Did God actually turn Enoch the man into Metatron the Archangel? In this book, you will read some of Metatron's own channeled words. He directly discusses his own nature, yet still allows all who read his words to draw their own conclusions. I appreciate the idea that Metatron was created by God as an angelic being and was given the rare opportunity to incarnate in human form, since I believe that all of us have a spiritual purpose to fulfill. Perhaps this is part of Metatron's purpose. You'll have to decide for yourself what you believe to be true.

If there is one thing Metatron does symbolize, however, it is balance. As humans, we walk a certain line every day—the line between our human nature and our spiritual nature. It isn't always easy to do the right thing when the alternative is simpler or more attractive. The great challenge we have in our lifetime is to keep our mind tuned in to spiritual matters and spiritual pursuits. The equilibrium that Metatron achieves in his own energy helps us recognize our own imbalances, and can show us how to start correcting them.

Let's examine Metatron's relationship to stability and unity a bit further.

Dual Natures

For me, being a mother to identical twin sons is both highly rewarding and challenging. When our boys were infants, my husband and I had to devise ways of telling them apart, usually dressing them in assigned colors and giving them pacifiers that matched their outfits. We only had to glance at the baby with the red binky to know he was Ben instead of Max. Now that they are older, it is much easier to tell them apart physically, but it is even simpler when you get to know their distinctive personalities. They may look alike, but they approach life in completely different ways. Thinking about my twins makes me appreciate even more some of the lore surrounding the Archangel Metatron.

Metatron stories often refer to his twin brother, the Archangel Sandalphon. The earliest tales claim that Sandalphon was the Biblical prophet Elijiah, who was elevated to angelic status in much the same way Enoch was. But no matter how he came into being, Sandalphon is always linked to Metatron as his twin. Most sources even mention their equal height, citing both of them as the tallest angels in the celestial kingdom. Sandalphon's main purpose seems to be to gather the prayers of those who believe into a tapestry or crown of energy, presumably for Creator.

As we noted earlier, Metatron has close associations with the Jewish mysticism of the Kabbalah, including its Tree of Life, a symbol of the creation of life and the interaction of its energies. The Western mystical tradition of Qabalah draws on the Jewish Kabbalah, along with astrology, tarot, alchemy, Gnosticism, hermeticism, and several other metaphysical philosopies, to ponder and investigate the nature of divinity. In Qabalastic interpretation, Metatron is the Archangel associated with Kether, the highest Sephirah, or sphere. This is the energy of the Beginning, the ultimate Force of God. Interestingly, Sandalphon is the Archangel connected to the last Sephirah, called Malkuth, which represents the energy of God manifesting in the physical world. In the diagram of the Tree of Life on page 26, you can see the paths that connect all the spheres. Notice the direct path in the middle pillar, from Kether at the top to Malkuth at the bottom? Isn't it interesting to see Metatron and his twin Sandalphon linked in this way? More important, this piece of Qabalistic information reinforces for us all that the path between humanity (in the physical world of Malkuth) and God (in the highest sphere of Kether) is always there. Our connection to the Divine is always present.

Not only does Metatron have a twin brother, he also has a female counterpart. In Hebrew lore, Metatron is associated with the Shekinah, the feminine side of God. In the Talmud, the Shekinah is purported to be present at times of group prayer, righteous judgment, and personal need. The Shekinah also seems to manifest at times of joy and creativity connected to spiritual aspirations. Thus, the Shekinah is often linked to the "Spirit of God." In Christian terms, this association could be taken one step further, coupling the Shekinah with the Holy Spirit, sometimes seen by more expansive Christians as the feminine nature of God the Father.

The Zohar, or *Book of Splendor,* offers more insight into Metatron and his association with Shekinah. The Zohar came to light in the early fourteenth century by way of Spanish Kabbalist Moses De Leon, who claimed the scrolls had been written 1,200 years earlier by Rabbi Simon, a disciple of Rabbi Akiva. Rabbi Akiva had allegedly entered Paradise to commune with God and then to convey his experiences to his followers. These were recorded and became known

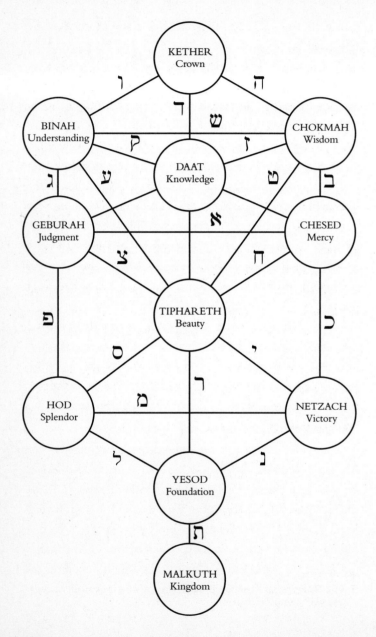

as the Zohar—although most likely De Leon himself wrote these scrolls.[7]

Nevertheless, in these writings, Metatron is closely associated with God, becoming the lesser God through his connection with the Tetragrammaton. Thus, Metatron is the male aspect of God, with the female aspect being Shekinah. According to the Zohar, the creation of the world is Shekinah's work. When Adam and Eve were banished from the Garden of Eden, some tales have Shekinah remaining there, while some have her wandering the earth along with the mother and father of humanity. Thus it becomes the quest of God's male aspect (Metatron) to reunite with God's female aspect (Shekinah) to bring balance to the Universe. Only through this unification can peace be achieved in all realms.

Inherent in Metatron's nature, then, are his role in helping balance the cosmos, and his dedication to helping humanity to achieve this on both a small scale (in daily life) as well as on a broader, more universal scale. We'll explore ways to do both later in the book. For now, let's look into some other esoteric thoughts associated with Metatron.

---

7 C. J. M. Hopking, *The Practical Kabbalah Guidebook* (New York: Sterling Publishing, 2001), 9.

Metatron's Cube

Another fascinating aspect of Metatron is his association with sacred geometry. According to one definition, sacred geometry is "an ancient science that explores and explains the energy patterns that create and unify all things and reveals the precise way that the energy of Creation organizes itself. On every scale, every natural pattern of growth or movement conforms inevitably to one or more geometric shapes."[8]

In other words, the study of sacred geometry leads one to an understanding of how Creator has structured the physical world around us. Within this plane, certain patterns emerge that point to its unity and connection to a Divine Mind that created it. Timeless geometric codes underlie seemingly disparate things, showing the parallels between patterns in snowflakes, shells, flowers, the corneas of our eyes, the DNA molecule that is the building block of human life, and the galaxy itself in which Earth resides. Further, ancient scholars believed that by studying sacred geometry and meditating on its patterns, inner knowledge of the Divine and our human spiritual progression can also be gained. These special sacred codes exist within humanity as well, emphasizing our link to Creator and our own Divine nature and purpose.

The Platonic Solids pictured here are the basis of sacred geometry, the five three-dimensional structures that are the foundation of all in the physical world.

---

8 LightSource Arts, "All of Creation Is Moving Light," www .sacred-geometry.com/sacredgeometry.html, accessed May 18, 2005.

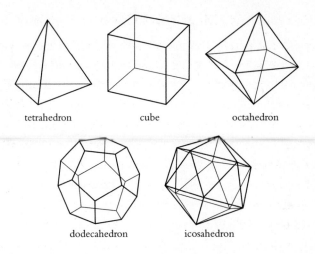

tetrahedron   cube   octahedron

dodecahedron   icosahedron

All are polyhedrons, that is, they are formed by multiple planes or faces. The tetrahedron has four faces: a familiar pyramidal shape. The cube is one type of hexahedron, a six-sided solid; other types are more oblong, with nonidentical planes. The octahedron has eight sides, the dodecahedron twelve, and the icosahedron twenty.

These Platonic Solids have been studied by scholars since the times of the Greek mystery schools nearly 2,500 years ago. The reality of this is being rediscovered in scientific thought, prompted in part by the work of the late Dr. Robert Moon of the University of Chicago, who postulated in the late 1980s that the entire periodic table of the elements is based on the Platonic Solids.

The Platonic Solids all occur in nature. For example, the cube, tetrahedron, and octahedron all appear in crystal formations. The methane molecule CH_4 is a tetrahedron with a central carbon atom and four hydrogen atomns at each corner. As we write with a pencil, the carbon atoms of the graphite crystals, arranged in hexagonal sheets, slice off to mark the paper. The vast majority of viruses are icosahedral, including the polio virus and the myriad cold viruses from which many of us suffer in the winter. The Platonic Solids have even been found in living sea creatures, in species of radiolaria. The dodecahedron-shaped *Circorrhegma dodecahedrus* is one example.

The Platonic Solids become even more powerful in esoteric thought when brought together to form Metatron's Cube, pictured here.

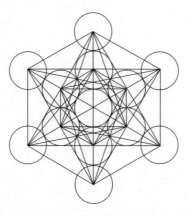

All of the Platonic Solids can be found within this structure, although it may be difficult to spot every one by looking at the flat image on a printed page. "Metatron's Cube represents the gridwork of our consciousness and the framework of our Universe," as one writer put it. "It is the Matrix in which everything is contained."[9] It also represents magick and alchemy, the manifestation of thought brought into the physical realm. Metatron's Cube helps us realize the harmony and balance of nature, since it depicts an equilibrium in the six directions represented within it. From this we can see why it is named for the Archangel most concerned with balance in all of nature.

Metatron's Cube is an excellent meditation tool. If you'd like to work with it, try the following exercise.

Choose a chair in a quiet area where you won't be disturbed. Turn off your phone and turn on some contemplative instrumental music that you enjoy. Take the image of Metatron's Cube and place or hang it where you can see it at eye level. Sit down and take several deep, cleansing breaths as you focus your eyes on the image. Allow your breathing to bring relaxation into your body. Keep your attention on the Cube and let any other thoughts that drift into your mind fade away without following them. Keep bringing your focus back to the image.

After a few moments, close your eyes. You will still be able to see the image in your mind. Keep concentrating on it, allowing thoughts to drift in and out of your head without becoming caught up in them. Your mind will begin to quiet as you focus on Metatron's Cube. Once your mind has settled and random thoughts have stopped flowing to you, keep breathing regularly, and ask Metatron in your

---

9 San Graal School of Sacred Geometry, "Alchemy, Magic, Incubation, Metatron, and Ancestors," www.sangraal.com/library/dedicated.htm, accessed Sept. 4, 2006.

mind if there is anything that you need to know at this time. Pay attention to any thoughts that come to you now, and know that you will remember these. Another image or vision may superimpose itself on the Cube, perhaps even taking its place completely. Observe everything that you see, feel, hear, and sense as you continue breathing. When the flow of information stops, thank Metatron for his input, and open your eyes. Write down everything you remember right away.

Metatron's Cube can be used as a visual focal point to connect with the Archangel, or it can be used as a concentration tool for meditations that promote peace and balance. Place an image of the Cube anywhere you wish to be reminded of the Archangel's loving, balancing presence.

Numerical Associations

Having learned about Metatron's connections with sacred geometry, perhaps you have already drawn conclusions concerning numerical associations as well. We've also learned about Metatron's parallels to the Egyptian deity Thoth, a god associated with geometry as well as writing and other disciplines. This connection, however, was not apparent to me until Metatron began impressing me with this information. Although I realize that geometry is a branch of mathematics, I still didn't put two and two together (no pun intended). I usually have to be hit upside the head with a metaphysical two-by-four to see these kinds of things. Metatron was happy to do that for me, God bless him.

As I started to organize my notes and thoughts concerning this book, I began to notice something: lots of elevens seemed to be cropping up in my life. Everywhere I looked, my eyes seemed to fall on this number. Clocks were constantly telling me it was 8:11, or 5:11, or, even more intriguingly, 11:11. I'd thumb through a book in a bookstore, and it would fall open to (you guessed it) page eleven. My sons' soccer jerseys, which I'd never paid close attention to before, screamed "11!" at me as I folded the laundry. It finally dawned on me that Metatron, my newest link to the angelic kingdom, was trying to clue me into something important. My training as a medium has taught me to pay attention to patterns and repetitions in my life, because these are often messages from the spirit realms that we need to unravel.

To research the number eleven and its esoteric implications, I turned to numerology, the metaphysical science of numbers and their energy. Viewed through this lens, every number is associated with specific vibrations. Let's take a brief look at the numbers one through nine and the personality attributes and qualities linked with them.

Number	Personality	Quality
1	Success-oriented, takes the lead, dominant, unique, lazy, overbearing	Will, spirit, masculine energies, creation
2	Cooperative, gentle, romantic, sympathetic, introspective, indecisive, fearful, dependent	Duality, feminine energies, truth, balance, peace, beauty
3	Joyful, versatile, witty, charming, social, ambitious, superficial, careless	Communication, independence, self-expression, expansion
4	Practical, organized, content, service-oriented, stingy	Discipline, grounding, matter and the material, Earth energies, the world, music
5	Restless, risk-taker, literary, traveler, sensual, irresponsible, anxious	Freedom, change, adventure, inspiration, adept
6	Romantic, wise, understanding, devoted, sexual, depressed, nosy	Love, the arts, union, ideals, nurturance, harmony
7	Reflective, passionate, intuitive, dreamy, solitary, pessimistic, moody	Mystical, philosophical, intellect, secret, life cycles
8	Materialistic, aggressive, persistent, zealous, greedy, militant	Authority, control, justice, karma, time, afterlife
9	Humanitarian, courageous, impulsive, compassionate, jealous, emotional	Universal consciousness, awareness, completion, the Higher Law

To determine someone's life path number, which will reveal the qualities she needs to master for success, first take her birth date, including the year she was born, and add all the numbers together. For example, I was born on

July 4, 1968. To find my life path number, add 7 (for July) plus 4 plus 1 plus 9 plus 6 plus 8 (use a calculator if you need to, as I do). This makes 35. Then add those individual digits together: 3 + 5 = 8. My life path number, then, is 8. Referring to the chart, I can read about that number's vibrational meaning and gain insights into my own attributes and challenges.

Now, let's say you were born on March 29, 1968:

$$3 + 2 + 9 + 1 + 9 + 6 + 8 = 38$$

and

$$3 + 8 = 11$$

Eleven is thought to be a master number, which means it contains its own vibration rather than the vibrations of the two numbers that comprise it. It is never broken down as "1 + 1 = 2." The master number 11 represents energies of intuition, psychic abilities, honesty, sensitivity, and idealism. "Eleven" energies are thought to be very connected with spirit and humanitarian ideals. Sounds angelic, doesn't it? Noteworthy as well is the fact that if you did break it into its base number (1 + 1 = 2), the 2 represents duality and balance, an attribute and energy we have already discussed in association with Metatron.

The appearance of a double eleven has great significance for some esoteric seekers. This combination of two master numbers side by side is thought to be a trigger placed into our cellular makeup prior to our decision to undertake a physical life. When this encoded message is "activated," it signifies that our time of ascension is near. Many think that when a person begins to see 11:11 on a regular basis in mundane life, it is a signal that a gateway is opening. For many, this gateway opens within the consciousness, a channel to the higher teachings and lessons on the functioning of the Universe and our human roles within it. It brings a deep understanding of the Divine nature of all, showing how we can overcome our humanness to reach our highest potential as spiritual beings.

In her book *Healing with the Angels,* angel expert and communicator Doreen Virtue discusses how angels send messages to human beings through the language of numbers. When we see sequences of ones or elevens, such as on clocks, says Virtue, an angel is impressing us to be very aware of our thoughts, which have a strong ability to manifest at this time. The ones and elevens notify the spiritual seeker that channels of opportunity are opening. By controlling negative thoughts and dwelling only on positive ones, the seeker can let wonderful things begin to happen.

Reading this interpretation of the number eleven reinforces for me its association with Metatron. I believe that Metatron has used the double-eleven in my life to remind me of his presence, and to impress upon me over and over again his connection to the Divine and to the balance that humanity naturally seeks to discover. So far no portals in the time-space continuum have swung open up for me, but I never rule out any possibility. I have confidence, though, that if you begin working with Metatron, he may use the number eleven to communicate with you as well. It is his gentle, loving way of expressing his willingness to connect with humanity, and reminding us how very connected we all are with Divinity.

————

As you have probably surmised by now, studying Metatron's background and the ancient stories surrounding him is an intriguing and thought-provoking process. And there is much, much more to learn about the Archangel, because the best knowledge always comes from our own personal, individual experiences. Metatron is waiting to get to know you on that level. Continue reading, and see what the Angel of the Presence has to reveal to you.

TWO

Personal Work with Metatron

Now that we've explored Metatron's history and connections to both our world and the Infinite, let's talk about some ways each of us can develop a personal relationship with this fascinating and powerful being. As with any meaningful friendship, it is important to concentrate on and cultivate this connection by making it a priority in your life.

One of the easiest things to do is to talk to Metatron. This may sound silly, but really, it is comforting to know he's only a thought away. Try speaking aloud to him when you're alone, and don't be afraid to talk about anything that comes to your mind. I often find myself talking to Metatron when I'm driving or when I'm cleaning up around the house. My body is engaged in doing something mundane, freeing my mind to think about any problems, concerns, or worries that I have. I've found that when I speak about these issues out loud to Metatron, not only do I feel better, but I often am impressed with a course of action that I can take to alleviate the issue.

Along with your challenges, you can also share your joys and celebrations with Metatron. Tell him about your promotion at work, about the terrific goal your son made at his soccer game, or about your wonderful weekend with that special new person in your life. Reviewing and reliving happy times helps elevate our moods and our energy vibrations, which can truly change our outlook on life in general. Metatron can work his angelic magic just by being a sounding board for you—take advantage of his available ear!

In this chapter you'll learn several exercises and activities that can bring you closer to Metatron's energy. I suggest you try them all and see which ones you enjoy the most. Each of us will gravitate toward certain activities, but we may never know which ones suit us best until we try each one in turn. If you have a less-than-impressive experience with an activity, I suggest trying it again at another time, just to be sure you didn't hit that exercise on a bad day. You may be surprised at which activities really resonate with you and which ones don't mesh with your energy.

I also suggest keeping a journal and taking the time after each activity to jot down some notes about your experience. This can help you track what exercises go well for you and which ones you'd like to try again. You may also want to note the day of the week, time of day, and moon cycle during which you attempt these various activities. Sometimes, the natural energies of the Universe, like the moon phase and time of day, can enhance or adversely affect an experience. We'll discuss this a bit more when we focus on ritual work, but the same can be true of the simpler exercises, too. A written record can help you see patterns in your work and can be a great asset when accessing Metatron's energy.

Meditations with Metatron

One of the best ways to get closer to the Archangel is through meditation. His powerful and loving presence can be felt and experienced any time you wish. Outlined here are several meditations that will help you get acquainted. First, let's review a few tips about meditation in general.

Meditation does not need to be difficult, but as a teacher I've found that many people have a tough time with it. I agree that it is sometimes hard to concentrate during a meditation, which is why it's a good idea to remove as many distractions as possible to get the full benefit of the experience.

First, find a comfortable spot for a seated meditation. Make sure the temperature suits you. Dim the lights and light a candle if you wish. Incense can also help to enhance the experience. Be sure to turn off the telephone and put the cat or dog in another room if your pet will distract you. (My dog likes to curl up in my lap when I meditate, and he seems to enjoy the quiet energy. Dogs, however, can suddenly jump up and bark if they hear noises, so use your best judgment.) If you have children, choose a time of day when they won't disturb you. Playing music, especially something angelic or classical, will draw Metatron's energy even closer to you.

I do recommend sitting up instead of lying down. We sleep in a reclining position, so naturally, the body and mind expect to sleep when we lie down. A seated position indicates to the mind and body that we are experiencing something other than sleep. Keep your spine straight, and try not to slouch in your chair. This opens up the trunk of your body and enhances breathing. Deep, steady breathing is the key to good meditation. When you breathe in, you should feel your stomach push out. This means you are using your diaphragm, which is essential to good cleansing and healing breathwork. When you exhale, push all the breath out of your body, beginning in the stomach area and working all the way up the torso until all the air has left your lungs. This is a full cycle of breath, and it enhances the meditation experience immeasurably.

Like any guided meditation, the ones outlined here can be read into a recording device and played back through headphones so that you can enjoy them over and over. This is especially helpful if you find your concentration wavering during your meditations.

Once the conditions in your meditation space are ready, you can sit down and start your connecting process. Breathe deeply and close your eyes. Concentrate on relaxing your body as you breathe, releasing stress and tension, and connecting with Metatron.

Note: Whenever you finish a meditation, especially an intense one, you might want to sip a glass of water and nibble a cracker or cookie to help ground your energy. It can be awkward to try to function after an especially powerful meditation and find that we can't focus on anything!

Pillar of Light Meditation

In many sources, Metatron is described as resembling a pillar of light or fire, in keeping with his role as an angel of the sun and of the element of fire. Fire is a purifying force; it burns away anything that is no longer needed. To work with Metatron requires a willingness to rid yourself of all energies that do not serve your own higher good or the will of Creator. Try this meditation to experience this cleansing in a way only Metatron can provide for you.

Breathe deeply, concentrating on relaxing your body. As you inhale, use your inner eyes and see the air enter your body as a stream of golden light. As you exhale, see the stress, tension, and negativity leave your body as a gray mist that dissipates immediately. Continue to breathe deeply, filling your whole being with the golden light of positive energy.

Now see before you a crystal staircase ascending to the heavens. Step up onto the first step—1—and feel your body lighten. As you continue climbing the crystal staircase—2—you feel your spirit lift. Step up—3—feeling closer and more connected to your Higher Power. Step up again—4—feeling lighter and lighter. Continue climbing higher—5—and step up again—6—feeling your heart lighten. Step up again—7—and feel your mind expanding, broadening, reaching out to Spirit that is all around you.

Continue climbing—8—feeling happiness and peace wash through you. Step up again—9—feeling yourself connect with all things, living and in Spirit, and continue moving up—10. One step remains, and as you step up—11—you feel relaxed, safe, connected with Creator, and in a deep state of peace and contentment.

Now see before you a brilliant Pillar of Light. The flames stretch so high that you cannot see the top of the pillar, and they burn with an intense golden light. You feel the warmth that emanates from this pillar, and you know in the deepest place in your heart that this is an incarnation of the Archangel Metatron. Your sense of peace and fulfillment deepens and expands as you stand in the presence of this amazing fire, and you feel blessed to be here. You begin walking toward the pillar, knowing that Metatron is beckoning you forward, welcoming you, inviting you to be in total concert with him.

Without hesitation, you step into the golden fire of the Pillar of Light, immersing yourself completely in its radiance and warmth. Immediately, you feel the light begin to heal you, going straight to any places in your body where healing energy is needed. Pain, stiffness, discomfort—all of these simply melt, recede, disappear, in the beneficent light of Metatron's true being. You are instantly whole.

Now, as you stand enveloped in the Archangel's fiery presence, you feel the intense healing of his nature enter your mind. All negative thoughts are instantly wiped from your consciousness and replaced with the burning passion of love. This is love for all things, all creatures, love for yourself and for all of Creator's magnificent beings. This is true cosmic love, the consciousness that we are all connected in the great circle of being that is Creator. Your mind opens and expands, understanding and compassion filling it with the most exquisite feeling of love you've ever experienced.

Metatron's consuming love spreads throughout your body and mind and into your soul. Your heart opens and connects with the Archangel, and you feel at peace with who and what you are. All questions, concerns, worries, and problems leave you as you realize that all is possible with Creator. Your soul recognizes its supreme task—to unite with and be free in Creator's love and peace. On every level, Metatron's purifying energy releases you from restriction and imbalance, leaving you with the undeniable sense that you are loved beyond measure, and that you are capable of displaying this very love in your life, in every way and in everything that you do.

Take as much time as you need to refresh yourself in this amazing presence. Know that Metatron and his powerful Fire of Love are always available to you at any time, whenever you need to be replenished. Understand that as you go forward, his strength and compassion will be with you always.

When you are ready to return to the current time and place, simply take a deep breath, thank Metatron for his healing, and open your eyes.

Healing Waters Meditation

Many of us struggle throughout our lives with self-esteem issues. You've probably heard someone say, "It's no wonder my spouse abandoned me. I'm unlovable." Perhaps a co-worker has uttered, "I'll never get anywhere in this company. I'm too stupid to learn these new skills." Maybe you've entertained similar thoughts, or ones like "I could never communicate with the angels or spirits. Why would they want to talk to someone like me?"

Stop this thinking immediately! Please realize how important and loved you are by Creator. You are a child of Divinity. As a member of this family, you are valued just as much as anyone else. If you have children of your own, you must be able to relate to this concept. No matter what our children do, we as parents continue to love them. The same is true of God on a scale infinitely larger and broader than we can fathom. God can no more stop loving us than we can stop loving our own children. In fact, the incredible love of Creator has the power to overcome any and all negative feelings, actions, emotions, and situations, no matter when they began. We are always welcome in God's house; we will never be abandoned for any reason.

Negative thinking about ourselves only serves one purpose: to drive us further away from Creator. If you want to be closer to God, and thus closer to the angels and spirit, you *must* reprogram your thinking to include only positive statements. If this seems like an insurmountable task, I assure you, it's not. And Metatron can help you do it.

As we know, one of the Archangel's greatest gifts to us is his understanding of human nature. He realizes how difficult it is to be human and to undergo the challenges of living in the world. He holds great compassion for us as beings struggling to connect with Creator. He also understands the feelings of unworthiness that plague so many of us. He wishes to help us overcome these negative thought patterns and strenghten our bond with Creator, thus elevating our existence and our spiritual direction.

Use the Healing Waters meditation when you are feeling emotionally disconnected, unloved, or unsure in your relationships with others or with God.

Sit in your special meditation spot and close your eyes. Begin taking slow, deep breaths, visualizing the air entering your body as a beautiful, cool blue light. This is the light of spiritual love and healing, positive and perfect. As you breathe out, see any negativity, pain, doubt, and fear leave your body as a gray mist that dissipates as soon as it is expelled. Continue breathing in and out for at least 11 cycles of breath, filling your body with the cool blue light of spiritual healing. Allow this light to encircle your body, like a robin's egg, completely surrounding you with its peaceful and protective presence. You feel safe and relaxed, safe and at peace.

Now see before you a crystal staircase ascending to the heavens. Step up onto the first step—1—and feel your body lighten. As you continue climbing the crystal staircase—2—you feel your spirit lift. Step up—3—feeling closer and more connected to your Higher Power. Step up again—4—feeling lighter and lighter. Continue climbing higher—5—and step up again—6—feeling your heart lighten. Step up again—7—and feel your mind expanding, broadening, reaching out to Spirit that is all around you. Continue climbing—8—feeling happiness and peace wash through you. Step up again—9—feeling yourself connect with all things, living and in Spirit, and continue moving up—10. One step remains, and as you step up—11—you feel relaxed, safe, connected with Creator, and in a deep state of peace and contentment.

At the top of the staircase, you see before you a shimmering cascade of clear water. This waterfall is so high, so broad, that you cannot see where it begins or how far it expands. Its colors are remarkably bright, amazing aquatic shades of blue, aquamarine, teal, azure, green, and violet. You can hear the sound of the water constantly moving, constantly replenishing itself, tumbling and churning in its own harmonious song. You realize as you watch the waterfall that you are in the presence of Metatron, manifested in his guise as an Angel of Emotional Balance, and you feel deeply moved in his presence. His energy feels cool and inviting, like a rejuvenating shower on a hot summer day, and you understand that he is inviting you to be replenished within his healing waters.

Without hesitation, you step forward, moving under the spray of the waterfall. Immediately, you are immersed in a sweet feeling of deep love. Coolness envelops you and washes over and through your entire being. Notice any areas in your body where the coolness seems to settle, where it directs special attention and energy. These are areas holding on to anger, negativity, resentment, or fear. Allow the healing waters to wash these negative feelings away, leaving only peace, serenity, happiness, and relief in their wake. (Pause for a few moments.)

Now, feel Metatron's cool, healing touch rise up to your solar plexus in the center of your abdomen. This is your seat of power, the place where your self-worth lies. Let the healing energy circulate here, like a small whirlpool of water, cleansing and opening this energy center. Listen as all negative statements about yourself are cleansed and released from your thinking and your truth. The healing energy swirls here, and as you listen, you hear a voice. It is no longer your own voice of fear and doubt, but the melodious, firm voice of Metatron himself: "You are loved. You are special. You are perfect. Believe." These phrases repeat over and over as the special healing waters continue to wash away all your remaining self-esteem issues and questions, leaving you feeling loved, feeling confident in yourself, and feeling safe in the Archangel's sweet and steadfast presence.

Remain in Metatron's healing waters for as long as you need to. He is always available to you at any time. Simply think of him, and he will be with you. And when you are ready to return to this time and space, breathe deeply, thank the Archangel for his help and guidance, and open your eyes.

Guarding Gaia Meditation

As one of the Angels of the Earth, Metatron has a special connection to our Earth Mother, also called Gaia in ancient traditions. Metatron is very concerned about the stewardship of the planet Earth and the need for all people who call Earth home to take responsibility for her maintenance and care. Unfortunately, many people today simply don't think about caring for our planet, our environment, and the other natural creatures and energies that inhabit Earth along with us. Enlisting the Archangel's powerful help and calling on his presence can help us remember the vital roles we play in maintaining a clean and healthy environment and helping raise others' awareness of these issues.

Try this meditation to connect with Metatron and further his efforts in caring for our Mother Earth.

Sit comfortably in your favorite meditation spot and center your consciousness to start relaxing. Begin your deep breath cycles, visualizing white light entering your body with every inhalation, and negativity, stress, and discomfort leaving your body as a gray mist with every exhalation. Breathe deeply for at least eleven cycles, feeling yourself become more peaceful and focused with each.

Now, in your mind's eye, see around your body a beautiful ring of vibrant green energy. It is like a hoop around you, pulsing with a steady, high frequency. You realize as you stand in this ring that you stand within the energy of the Archangel Metatron, in his guise as an Angel of Gaia. You understand that this green ring of cosmic fire is healing energy, and as one of God's precious creations, you are as entitled to this gift of healing as any other. Take a moment to allow this healing energy to bathe your body, especially letting it soak into the areas of your life that need healing. (Pause for a few moments.)

Now see Metatron's ring of healing energy begin to expand. As it moves outward, you see that you are no longer alone in the circle of energy. All around you, you notice animals, birds, waters containing fish and sea life, insects, and other living creatures. You see plants, trees, grass, flowers, all manner of vegetation that populates and beautifies the Earth. You see streams, rivers, lakes, and oceans, and you see beaches, deserts, rainforests, mountaintops, canyons . . . all breathtakingly beautiful, and now all surrounded by the vibrant green light. You understand that Metatron's energy is protecting these natural gifts, and his healing is repairing the damage done by humankind to these places and species that need caretaking.

As the ring of green healing energy continues to expand, you see human beings within it, too. As you look at each one, you see that the green energy has settled in each person as a light in the center of the chest, nestled in the heart chakra. You realize that Metatron is opening this chakra with his healing and compassionate presence, nurturing within that heart the desire and the understanding necessary to take care of the planet Earth and all her creatures and resources. You feel your own heart chakra begin to expand, warm, and vibrate as the essence of the healing energy takes hold in you. (Pause for a few moments.)

And now it is time to release the energy into the Universe. As the ring expands and disappears, you know that the healing has taken place, and that the Archangel has brought to humankind the compassion it needs to take responsibility for the Earth. His healing energy will continue to permeate the natural world and the hearts of human beings who are open to receive it.

When you feel ready, open your eyes. You are relaxed and at peace, safe and secure in your knowledge and your trust in Metatron.

Violet Wind Meditation

Metatron has a deep connection to Creator, and, as such, is one of the Angels of Prayer. There are myriad ways to pray—more than many people realize—and many ways in which prayers may be answered. Prayer can be utilized to worship, to praise, to thank, to petition, or simply to draw closer to God. When we pray, we put our trust in Creator; we trust that we will be heard and answered in some way. It is sometimes hard, however, to understand the answers that are brought to us. We may miss important information that God sends in answer to our prayer simply because we don't know how to interpret the messages that are broadcast. Connecting to Metatron can enhance our ability to communicate and understand these messages.

Use the Violet Wind meditation to strengthen this vital tie to God.

Relax in your special meditation space and begin deep breathing. As you breathe in, see a cleansing white light entering your body. As you breathe out, see any negativity, pain, or stress leaving your body as a cloud of gray mist that dissipates into the ethers, transmuted into something positive. Keep breathing as the white light fills your body.

After eleven cycles of breath, open your mind's eye to visualize. See before you a crystal staircase ascending to the heavens. Step up onto the first step—1—and feel your body lighten. As you continue climbing the crystal staircase—2—you feel your spirit lift. Step up—3—feeling closer and more connected to your Higher Power. Step up again—4—feeling lighter and lighter. Continue climbing higher—5—and step up again—6—feeling your heart lighten. Step up again—7—and feel your mind expanding, broadening, reaching out to Spirit that is all around you. Continue climbing—8—feeling happiness and peace wash through you. Step up again—9—feeling yourself connect with all things, living and in Spirit, and continue moving up—10. One step remains, and as you step up—11—you feel relaxed, safe, connected with Creator, and in a deep state of peace and contentment.

At the top of the crystal staircase, pause and look around. See before you a beautiful meadow of flowers. They are white, stretching as far as you can see into the distance like a blanket of snow. Move into the field of flowers, enjoying their beauty. Standing in the midst of them, you feel a soft wind begin to blow. As you feel it caress your cheek, you notice that you can see this wind; it is a lovely shade of violet. It curls gently around you, moving all around your body in a dance of color and motion. You realize as you feel and watch that this is the Archangel Metatron in his guise as an Angel of Prayer, an Angel of the Air, who has come to help you connect more closely with Creator.

As you stand, you feel the wind encircle the trunk of your body, right above your navel. You feel concentrated energy in this spot, the solar plexus, the seat of power for all people and the center of clairsentience, clear feeling. Metatron's violet light pulsates here, blending with the yellow light of the solar plexus, strengthening it, making it brighter. The solar plexus chakra opens like a flower of stunning yellow light, and you understand that you will feel the answers to the questions you bring to God in prayer much more easily, and that you will trust these feelings as truths for you and your situation.

You feel Metatron's wind move up your body to encircle your throat, pulsing as it surrounds your throat chakra. This is the seat of clairaudience, the ability to hear messages. The violet light blends with the bright blue of the throat chakra, enhancing its color. The throat chakra spins and opens like a blooming flower, and you understand that you will hear answers to your prayer with your inner ears, the clairaudient ears that pick up Spirit's voice.

Metatron's wind moves up your body again, encircling your head, pulsating over the spot in your forehead between your eyes. This is your third eye, the center of clairvoyance, clear vision, the ability to see picture messages. The violet light blends with the indigo light of the third eye chakra, making it glow even more brilliantly. The chakra spins and opens, and you understand that you will see symbols and pictures that will answer any questions you bring to God in prayer.

Stand and enjoy the new energy brought to you by the Archangel and his healing wind. Know that your chakras, your energy centers, have been opened and enhanced to let more information come to you from Creator in answer to your prayers. Know that this Divine connection can be honed anytime you wish simply by reconnecting with Metatron in this way.

Take as much time as you want to enjoy Metatron's presence, and when you feel ready, begin to feel your body again. Begin to tune back in to the room around you, to this time and space. When you're ready, open your eyes, relaxed and refreshed.

Akashic Records Meditation

One of Metatron's most prominent roles is as the Angel of the Akashic Records. These records are the Universe's energetic repository of all actions, thoughts, and information from the beginning of time. They are accessible to all of us as spiritual beings inhabiting a physical body, and we can work with Metatron to help us access this information to better ourselves in our current life circumstances.

Try this meditation to become more familiar with the Akashic Records and the Archangel's connection to them.

Go to your meditation spot and begin by closing your eyes. Breathe deeply and visualize your breath entering your body as a beautiful, clear white light. This is positive energy, strength, and relaxation. As you exhale, see your breath leaving your body as a gray mist that dissipates into the atmosphere. This mist is negative energy, stress, and pain. As you continue breathing in and out, your body fills with white light, relaxing and feeling better and better. Continue breathing for eleven cycles.

Now see in your mind's eye the crystal staircase that ascends into the heavens. Step up onto the first step—1—and feel your body lighten. As you continue climbing the crystal staircase—2—you feel your spirit lift. Step up—3—feeling closer and more connected to your Higher Power. Step up again—4—feeling lighter and lighter. Continue climbing higher—5—and step up again—6—feeling your heart lighten. Step up again—7—and feel your mind expanding, broadening, reaching out to Spirit that is all around you. Continue climbing—8—feeling happiness and peace wash through you. Step up again—9—feeling yourself connect with all things, living and in Spirit, and continue moving up—10. One step remains, and as you step up—11—you feel relaxed, safe, connected with Creator, and in a deep state of peace and contentment.

At the top of the crystal staircase, pause and look around. You are in a beautiful, peaceful clearing, filled with a serene energy. Before you, you see a large glass building on the far shore of a babbling stream. From inside the building, a bright golden light emanates, a light that seems to beckon you inside. You cross the stream and climb the steps into the glass building, eager to see what lies inside.

Once inside, you immediately realize you have entered a sacred place. The golden light touches everything inside the building, and you feel washed in its essence, preserved and protected by it. The hall seems to ring with melodious music, and this lifts your spirit even higher. You understand that this is the well-known Hall of Records, where the Akashic Records are kept, and that this golden light permeating it is the Archangel Metatron.

As you look around, you notice that, as far as you can see, shelves line the walls of the building, and massive books rest on these shelves. These are the Records that tell of everything the world has ever known, and the vibrations that were created to make the world what it will be in the future. These books are accessible to all people who approach them with respect and love and open them with good intentions, with the desire to make the world a better place. The Archangel knows that you have a special concern right now, one you're seeking insight about. Take a moment to think about this situation and ask a pertinent question about it. (Pause.)

Now, look around and notice that one book has been taken off the shelf and laid open on a nearby table. Metatron has brought you an answer to your question. Approach the book and look inside. Perhaps you will read words that are meaningful to you. Perhaps you will see symbols or pictures that could lead you to an answer. Maybe you will feel a sense of peace, or maybe you will suddenly understand a course of action as you look into the book. Whatever you see, read, or feel, you will remember, and you will be able to apply this to your problem for a viable solution.

When you have finished looking at the book, step back and thank Metatron for his intervention. If you need help in the future, you can always return to this place and call on him as you access the Records again.

Now it is time to begin the journey back. You leave the Hall of Records and cross back over the stream to the crystal staircase. As you descend from the eleventh step to the first, you become more aware of your physical body and surroundings, until finally, on the number 1, you open your eyes, wide awake and at peace, remembering everything you've experienced.

Now sit down and write some notes about your experience with the Akashic Records. If you were shown symbols in the book, they may not make sense to you right away. Sometimes, messages become clearer as we think them over, draw associations, and contemplate how certain images or words may be applied in our lives. Whatever you were shown, however, will have pertinence to your situation. You just have to figure out what the meanings are. And you can always ask Metatron to help you interpret your message, too!

Tools for Working with Metatron

Tools make our lives easier. Just think how much harder it would be to cook dinner without the many tools we use in the kitchen. Can you imagine trying to mash potatoes without a masher? Ingeniously, humanity has invented many such gadgets to help us with the challenges of cooking, cleaning, and otherwise running our everyday lives.

Spiritual tools are no different. As a student of Wicca, I learned how to use a wand to direct energy, how to sever energy using an athame or sword, and how to charge certain objects to hold special energies. By doing this, we can connect more easily to the astral planes and access other energies that we wish to manipulate or understand.

Cleansing and consecrating tools also gives us a physical representation of the energy with which we forge our connection. Spiritual tools become a tangible reminder of our concentration on our spiritual studies and path. They help us to stay focused and centered in a world filled with distractions and negative energy. By holding fast to the tools we create, we can find a respite from the chaos of the everyday world.

Let's look at several suggestions for tools to cleanse, consecrate, and charge with Metatron's special energy. These tools can help bring the Archangel's energy closer to you every day and remind you of his presence and constant readiness to help as you go about your daily business.

METATRON CRYSTAL

I love crystals and gemstones. Not only are they beautiful, but each contains a wonderful energy that can be harnessed for beneficent reasons. All stones possess a subtle yet powerful vibration and purpose that we can access to improve our circumstances: to promote physical healing, to open ourselves psychically, for mental and spiritual therapy, and for many other reasons. Amethyst, for example, can be used to enhance psychic visions, but it is also a great stone for warding off negative energy. Rose quartz can help people who have self-esteem issues, and citrine can attract money and prosperity. The many stones that decorate our earth also have myriad attributes; we need only take the time to learn about them.

One popular and incredibly versatile stone is quartz crystal. Quartz carries many positive attributes, but one of its most amazing is the ease with which it can be programmed. Programming a crystal is the meditative process by which a person instructs the crystal on the tasks and energies for which it will be used. Because quartz crystal is a natural amplifier, it heightens and enhances any programming given to it, thus making those energies easier to access. For example, you can program a quartz crystal to amplify your clairvoyant abilities. Once the crystal has been programmed this way, keeping it nearby while doing readings for other people or while meditating for personal visions increases those appearances.

In this same way, a quartz crystal can be programmed to enhance your communication with the Archangel Metatron.

First, you will need a quartz crystal. This alone may seem like a daunting project. If you have ever browsed through a shop displaying crystals, the various sizes, shapes, and price tags may dazzle you. Don't let yourself be intimidated or overwhelmed. Shopping for a Metatron crystal should be fun! Simply ask the Archangel to accompany you and influence you in your choice of a crystal to use in communications with him. He will be more than happy to aid you in your selection. And if you have no idea where to go to purchase a stone, get out the telephone book, ask for Metatron's assistance, and look up gem, stone, crystal, or mineral shops in your area. Many New Age and esoteric boutiques also carry crystals, so locate those as well.

If unsure, make some phone calls before taking a trip. (Do go to an actual store so you can experience the energies of the crystals. Online shopping is a convenience, but you can't touch or hold the crystals you're considering before placing your order. Buy online only if shopping in a store is impossible for you.)

As a student of esoteric knowledge, one of the most important things you'll ever learn is to discern between different and quixotic energies. Choosing stones is one way to experience many types of energies and learn which vibrations fit best with your own.

I recommend choosing a stone no larger than the palm of your hand. If you'd like something smaller, that's fine, but stay away from the tiny quartz shards that are sometimes sold. These can be very fragile, and since you'll be handling your crystal quite often, look for more durability. Once you have found some quartz crystals that seem to be the right size, notice which ones attract you the most. Take a few moments to hold each of these in your hand. Focus on your breathing as you hold each one in turn, closing your eyes if it helps you concentrate. Which ones feel the best in your hand? Which make you feel calm and centered versus anxious or nervous? When you say the name Metatron in your mind, which seem to grow warmer? Narrow down your choices using these questions and methods until only one crystal remains. Now, you've got the perfect quartz crystal to program for Metatron!

When you get home, you need to cleanse your crystal. This process really has nothing to do with dirt or dust.

Everything around us carries energy vibrations, and any object can pick up vibrations from its environment. Gemstones and crystals are especially susceptible to the influence of subtle energies and can carry negative vibrations. By ridding your crystal of these vibrations, you will let it function for you at the highest level possible.

To cleanse your stone, soak it in a mixture of fresh water and sea salt for several hours. In her book *Love Is in the Earth: A Kaleidoscope of Crystals,* author Melody recommends soaking gemstones for twelve hours to rid them of unwanted energies. Metatron tells me a crystal intended to enhance communication with him can be soaked for eleven hours. Do what feels best to you.

After soaking your crystal, remove it from the water, dry it, and then allow it to charge in the sun for another hour. I usually put my crystals on a plate or in a basket and set them outside on my patio to soak up the sun's energy. You can lay yours on a windowsill if you don't wish to put it outside. After your crystal has sunbathed, it is ready to be programmed.

Take your crystal to your meditation space and get comfortable in your favorite spot. Play angelic music and burn a white or gold candle if you want to further set the mood. Hold the crystal in your dominant hand and close your eyes.

Breathe deeply as you do in preparation for meditation, centering yourself. See in your mind a beautiful bright white light. See yourself standing within this light, holding your crystal. Know that this white light is the love energy of the Universe, the God-force manifested as light. You are safe and protected within it.

Now, within your mind, call to the Archangel Metatron. As you do this, see the light's color change to gold. You now stand in the presence of Metatron, and you feel comfortable and peaceful with him. As you hold your crystal, let the golden light of his essence wash over and through it, making it glow like a beacon. The crystal becomes warmer in your hand. Hold in your mind the absolute intention of enhancing your communication with Metatron. Think to yourself, "I program this crystal to increase my ability to hear, see, and understand Metatron's presence and messages in my life." Know without a doubt that this is so.

Continue to concentrate on strengthening your crystal's programming for at least several minutes. When you feel ready, thank Metatron for his presence and then open your eyes. Put your newly programmed crystal in a special place where it will remind you of the connection you have made to the Archangel.

Now you can use your crystal in a variety of ways. Carry it with you on days when you need an extra boost of angelic energy. My Metatron crystal is fairly large, but I have smaller gemstones I carry with me for various reasons in small suede pouches in my purse. If your crystal is small enough, you can even slip it into your trouser pocket to take with you to work or school. One of my friends has been known to carry small crystals in her brassiere! Just remember, ladies: if you bend over, they can come tumbling out, so use your best judgment. And hey—maybe that's Metatron's way of getting you to laugh!

Since you programmed your crystal to enhance your communication with Metatron, use it during your meditations. Hold your stone in your left hand while deep breathing to relax and center. Why the left hand? Our left side is the receptive half of our body; the right side gives energy out to others and to the Universe. By holding the crystal in your left hand, you are further opening yourself to receive stronger messages. Ask Metatron to be with you in your meditation. If specific questions are plaguing you, ask him for guidance. Remember, no problem is too great or too small. Once you have asked the question, pay close attention to any thoughts, sounds, images, or feelings you have immediately afterward. These are the answers! They may be symbolic, so when you finish your meditation, write down anything that came to you in response to your questions. Analyze the symbols to decipher the message Metatron sent to you.

Your crystal can also enhance your communication with Metatron through your dreams. Dreams are an esoteric bridge to the higher planes, and the Archangel can speak to you through yours. (For more on interpreting dreams, see page 82.)

As you ready yourself for sleep, hold your crystal and concentrate on an issue or problem for which you need guidance. Ask Metatron to send you messages in your dreams to help solve this dilemma. Set the crystal on your nightstand next to your bed, or place it in a sack and put it under your pillow before retiring. Keep a notebook or recording device next to your bed, too, so that as soon as you awaken, you can record what you remember from your dream. Images,

colors, feelings, concepts, conversation: record it all immediately, whatever the time of night. Even if you have a good
memory, you will probably forget some details if you wait
until later—so don't risk missing your guidance by neglecting your part of the process! If you're worried about disturbing your bed partner, write in the dark, or sleep in another
room on the nights you are seeking guidance. After you have
it all down, go back and consider the symbols and meanings you see in your notes. (This can be done later if need
be.) Your answer will be there, hidden in the shorthand language of angelic communication. Or, if you get lucky, you
may simply awaken with a knowing, a firm understanding,
of the answer to your problem. Be sure to thank Metatron
for his assistance.

The crystal can also be used for healing work. Even if
you are not a healer yourself, Metatron can help you heal
on physical, emotional, or spiritual levels. Of course, he also
wants you to take good care of your body, so if you have
a serious condition, please see your doctor and do everything you can within the realms of science and medicine
to get the help you need.

To experience Metatron's healing energy, use your crystal. Lie down comfortably and place the crystal on the part
of your body that troubles you. You can also lie on top of
the crystal if you are having trouble with your back, neck,
or any back-of-the-body areas: wrap the stone in a towel
or washcloth and tuck it under the area. Take several deep
breaths and ask for Metatron to surround you with his presence. Let yourself relax as you breathe and ask Metatron to
bring healing to you where your physical body needs it.

Concentrate and notice any sensations in your body. You may feel warmth or tingling, or perhaps a chill or tightening. Relax into the sensation and let Metatron bring healing to you, knowing that this is happening and that it is always for your best and highest good.

If you need emotional healing, lie down and place your crystal on your heart chakra in the center of your chest. As before, relax into your deep breathing and focus on Metatron's presence. Petition him to bring you the emotional healing and release you need to be well again. Continue to concentrate on this until you feel more at peace.

Do you need spiritual healing? Engage the crown chakra, which is at the top of our head, connecting us all to Creator. Do as described above for emotional healing, but this time sit up with the crystal resting on top of your head. If this is uncomfortable, simply lie down and place the crystal right next to the crown of your head. Again, concentrate on Metatron as you breathe and relax, and ask him to bring peace and guidance to you on your spiritual issues.

Using your Metatron crystal can help you make better food choices, too. I'll be the first to admit to eating junk food, especially when I'm bored or worried. Like all angels, Metatron wants the best for humanity and recognizes the problems that poor nutrition can cause. Place your Metatron crystal in your kitchen in a prominent place. As you position it, ask Metatron to remind you to eat only healthy foods. The next time you go into the kitchen to sneak an Oreo or another glass of soda, don't be surprised when your eyes fall on the crystal, and a little voice inside your head reminds you to watch your intake of empty calories!

You can also use the crystal to infuse your beverages with high angelic energy. This works best with spring water. Simply fill a glass with water and drop your crystal into it. As you hold the glass, ask Metatron to bless your water and fill it with his energy for your highest and best good. Drink, then remove the crystal and let it dry on a towel. After imbibing, you may find that many of your thoughts are loving and peaceful throughout the day. Metatron brings a special magick to everything he touches.

These are just some of the ways you can use your Metatron crystal to connect more frequently with the Archangel's energy. I'm sure you can think of many other ways to bring his wonderful energy closer to you every day. Enjoy your unique, sparkling crystal link to Metatron!

INFUSIONS AND HERBS

Our sense of smell has powerful effects on the body and mind. Although not as strong in human beings as in some of our animal counterparts, it is still considered by scientists to be a vital component of our human nature. Research shows that anosmics (people who have partially or fully lost their sense of smell) are prone to depression, and that their quality of life is severely affected.[1] It has also been suggested that smell can influence our moods and emotions, our memories, our health, and even our choice of mate! Incorporating scent into our esoteric work can only enhance our understanding of the world (and the other worlds) around us.

---

1 "Smell and Taste and Anosmia," Tim Jacob's Research and Teaching Information, Cardiff University website, www.cf.ac.uk/biosi/staff/jacob/teaching/sensory/olfact1.html.

In my work as a massage therapist, I use essential oils to facilitate a more relaxing and healing experience for my clients. Although the topical massage oil I prefer is unscented, I usually add a few drops of eucalyptus oil to my bottle to help relax tight muscles even further. I dress the face cradle of my massage table with eucalyptus for clients who have breathing or allergy issues so that they can lie prone without becoming congested. Several drops of lavender oil on the sheets can induce further relaxation, making my job easier as I work to loosen muscle groups. Recently, I found an infusion of rose water at a local healing center, and I now enjoy spraying this in the air of my office before conducting clairvoyant readings or teaching sessions. Rose oil attracts very high-energy vibrations, and it seems to bring a truly heightened sense of divinity when I am working. Clients often comment on how tranquil they find my workspace to be.

Preparing your own scented infusion can further enhance your connection to the Archangel Metatron. It is fairly simple to make, costs little, and smells wonderful! Purchase a small bottle with a spray top and fill it with about four ounces of distilled water. Add the following essential oils to the bottle (no more than ten drops per four ounces of water):

- nutmeg

- myrrh

- lavender or lily of the valley

- sea salt (a pinch) for purification

Shake your infusion to mix the ingredients. Spray it in your meditation space before making your connections with Metatron. Try using it when you are faced with a particularly challenging situation or before going to work in the morning to remind yourself of Metatron's presence and willingness to help. Before retiring, mist your bedclothes and pillowcases with it to help connect to the Archangel in your dreams. I'm sure you'll think of many ways to use your Metatron Mist to uplift and inspire!

You can also use dried herbs to create an environment welcoming to Metatron. A pretty bowl displayed prominently in your home is perfect for a mixture of herbs that resonate with his energy. Not only will the herbs scent your house, they will remind you of your connection to the Archangel. Try the following mixture, which in these measurements covers the bottom of a saucer:

- three to five nutmeg pieces
- spearmint
- sandalwood
- dragon's blood oil (to bind)

Grind the nutmeg into a powder using a mortar and pestle. Add two to four pinches of spearmint and sandalwood. Bind with three to four drops of dragon's blood. Mix together, transfer to a small bowl or container, and set in your meditation space or bedroom.

Edible herbs can also be added to your favorite dishes to remind you of Metatron's importance in your life. Try the following to connect with the many aspects of Metatron's influence:

- Air aspects: fennel, parsley, dill, oregano

- Fire aspects: sunflower, garlic, onion

- Earth aspects: bee pollen, betel nuts, ginseng, sea salt

- Water aspects: lettuce, apple, vanilla

It might be fun to prepare a whole meal devoted to Metatron. What dishes can you think of that may highlight his attributes? The Archangel can help bring balance to your eating habits, lifestyle choices, and all health matters. It may be beneficial to explore the idea of setting a menu that Metatron helps you select.

CANDLES

I love working with candles. In my many years of Wiccan study, no spellwork resonated more for me than candle magick. Candles are inexpensive, accessible, and can be used over and over again for connection work. They are also fun to make and can become powerful tools when charged with a specific intention.

Indeed, just like the other tools we've discussed so far, candles can be charged to carry certain energies. The great thing is that once those energies are infused into the candle, it can be burned, releasing those energies into the Universe and drawing in your intention. Candles can be used to bring healing to someone's life, to draw prosperity to a home, or to protect a loved one. The uses of candle magick are as myriad as its practitioners! And candles can be the perfect vehicle to strengthen your connection to Metatron.

So how do you get started? The most important thing you'll need is a candle, of course. The type of candle you select is up to you; here are a few factors to consider.

What size candle should I choose? I prefer to work with thicker candles, rather than skinny tapers. Depending on my intention, I use a variety of sizes, from votive candles to huge three-wick pillars. For your Metatron candle, you might prefer one that is a bit bigger so that it lasts longer.

What color is best? Certain colors carry particular energies, so color is key when selecting a candle for magickal work. Metatron is an Angel of the Sun, associated with the energies represented by that heavenly body, those of recognition, will, and success. Yellow and gold candles seem to resonate with Metatron's energy. Yellow candles correspond with attraction and communication, gold ones with confidence and courage. Either will work well. If you can't find a yellow or gold candle, or if you're in a pinch and can't get to the store, a white candle will substitute just fine. The color white is associated with Divine Energy, and white can be used for any intention when performing candle magick.

Should I buy natural candles? Some practitioners insist on using only natural ingredients in their magickal work, including candles. Beeswax and soy candles are available for those who prefer to use them. I have not found an energetic difference between natural candles and those with man-made ingredients, but everyone must judge and do for herself. If you like natural candles, use them.

When should I work with the candle? On a Sunday, ideally. Sundays correspond to Metatron's energy as an Angel of the Sun, and I've found them best for connecting with his general presence. Try to choose a Sunday when the moon is waxing (getting larger) or when the moon is full. Remember that moon phase energy lasts for three days on either side of the phase's fullest point. For instance, if your calendar depicts the full moon on a Friday, the full moon energy actually lasts from the previous Tuesday to the following Monday. This will be good energy in which to create your Metatron candle, ideally on the Sunday in that range.

You will also need these supplies:

- a candle holder that fits your chosen candle. Brass or another metal is best, since wooden candleholders may catch fire, and glass may crack with heat.

- a nail, small penknife, or other carving tool

- essential oil (nutmeg, myrrh, lavender, dragon's blood)

- matches or a lighter

Take your candle and your supplies to a place where you won't be disturbed. If you can do this in the space where you meditate with Metatron, so much the better. You might prefer to work at a table or other flat, stable surface. Note: never leave a candle burning unattended in your home.

First, take your candle in your hands and close your eyes. Center yourself and take some long, cleansing breaths until you feel peaceful and relaxed. Now envision yourself in a bright circle of white light. This is the protection and love of the Divine Consciousness, encircling you so that you are safe and at peace. Know in your heart that you are connected to Creator and thus to everything in the Universe.

Envision your candle and, in your mind, ask that all negative or unproductive energy in the candle be released at this time. Watch as this unwanted energy begins to drain from the candle in the form of gray mist. Know that as this energy dissipates, the Universe transforms it into positive vibrations.

Now, as you watch in your mind's eye, see the candle begin to glow with positive energy. Watch as it fills with the same beautiful, bright white light of the Divine that surrounds you. Feel it become warm in your hands as you hold it, as it becomes as bright as a small sun. Know that this candle now contains the powerful, positive love energy of the Universe.

Open your eyes, take up your nail or penknife, and begin to think about the Archangel Metatron and your desire to communicate with him. Concentrate on this as you carve Metatron's name into the surface of the candle. You can carve other words, too, if you wish, like *connect, communicate, hear, see, understand,* or anything else that describes the relationship you seek with him. You may want to carve symbols or pictures on the candle as well: perhaps a heart to remind you of Metatron's love, or an arrow to represent swift messages. Keep concentrating on this wish to communicate. If you find your mind wandering as you carve, gently bring it back to focus. Continue carving until you are satisfied with the words and symbols you have chosen.

Now it is time to dress your candle with essential oil. (You may want to wear gloves for this step; essential oils can be absorbed through the skin, and some are harmful. I have not had trouble with any of the oils mentioned, but please use your own best judgment.) Put a few drops of oil on your fingertips and, starting at the top of your candle, rub the oil downward, stopping in the middle. Dress all the way around the candle in the same fashion. Then, turn the candle and rub oil up from the bottom of the candle to meet in the middle. You always dress a candle in this fashion if you wish to draw something toward you. Remember to concentrate on your desire to communicate with Metatron as you dress your candle.

Then set your candle securely in its holder and wash your hands before lighting it. Some people prefer matches, others lighters, because of the energies associated with them. I have heard that angels do not like the sulphur from matches, but I have not found it to be a problem. I usually use wooden kitchen matches, and I've never had a problem calling in any angel, let alone Metatron. Use what feels best to you.

As you light your candle, invoke the Archangel using a special prayer or petition. Write one of your own, or try something like this:

> *In this time and in this hour,*
> *I call to Metatron and his power*
> *Of preserving love and bringing peace.*
> *Great Metatron, may you never cease*
> *To be with me through trials and pain*

To remind me of Creator's love again.
Thank you for your presence here.
Please stay with me, Archangel dear.

Since you have created this candle exclusively to invoke Metatron's presence, it may be burned again and again when you need to focus on his special energy. You may choose to burn it while meditating with Metatron, or while working with him in other ways. You might burn it when you need extra help with a certain problem. Light the candle, use your Metatron invocation, and then tell the Archangel all about the issue. You don't have to use fancy words; he will understand no matter what you say. And if you ask for his help in resolving the problem, don't be surprised when a solution presents itself, even if it's not the one you imagined. Sometimes our spirit helpers know much better what we need than we do. Don't forget to thank Metatron for his assistance, too.

When you are finished burning your candle, snuff it or pinch it out. Magickal tradition frowns on blowing out a flame, believing that this scatters the magickal energy infused in the candle. Candlesnuffers are easily found at shops, or you can use an old metal spoon. Some people are adept at clapping their hands over a candle flame to extinguish it, or at wetting the thumb and forefinger and pinching the flame out. I have never been good at either one, so I snuff my candles. Again, the choice is yours.

Another way to invoke Metatron's powerful assistance is by using petition magick along with your candle. This method works well for issues that may need more time to manifest, such as a job search or working toward saving money for an expensive item. Define what it is you need by brainstorming and jotting down ideas on a piece of paper. When you have all of your thoughts down, try to pull them together into one cohesive thought that can be written on a single slip of paper. For instance, let's say you are frustrated in your current position at work and feel a new job would be beneficial. When you brainstorm, think about all of the aspects of your current job that you would like to change for the better. When you're finished, your list may read something like this:

> Better salary
> Better health benefits
> More vacation time
> Flexible hours
> Happy, productive co-workers
> An office with a window

OK, that last one may seem silly or trite, but if it's important to you, if it's something you would truly like to change, then add it to your list! Don't limit yourself, and don't limit what the Universe can bring to you.

Now gather all these items together and state them as a single, positive sentence about what you are seeking—framed as if you already have it! For this example, you may try something like:

> *I have a new job with the perfect pay and benefits, flexible work hours, generous vacation time, happy, productive co-workers, and an office with a window.*

Do you see how this sentence is constructed in a way that tells the Universe that this situation has already manifested? *This is vital to your success!* You must see and believe that you deserve this situation and can have it before you can expect it to manifest in your life. Metatron is powerful and wants to help you with any and all issues, but if you do not see yourself as successful, you will not be. Metatron may have to spend all of his time boosting your sense of self-worth first before anything else can manifest!

To draw an item or a situation to yourself, state what you desire in a clear and logical form. *I have a new job* tells the Universe exactly what you are seeking, and it also pointedly states that this new position will come without causing you any grief or tension. Then, the statement goes on to list the job qualities being sought, clearly and confidently. The request is short, to the point, and positive, all the components that attract the most beneficial energies.

Once you have written your positive statement or affirmation, copy it in big, bold letters on an index card or a clean sheet of paper. If you want to add even more energy to it, write in red ink for swift action, purple to channel success and higher powers, or gold for the Archangel Metatron. Decorate it with star stickers, or draw colorful flowers or symbols that represent to you the petition you've made. The more energy you put into the magick, the more energy you will get back from it.

Finally, take your petition to your Metatron candle. Say your Metatron invocation and light your candle, welcoming the Archangel. Take a few moments to commune with him in meditation. When you feel connected, tell him that you have an issue with which you would like his help. Hold your petition and read it aloud to Metatron, knowing without a doubt that he hears and understands your request. Then place the petition under the candle holder. Spend a few more moments in meditation, visualizing yourself acquiring the situation or item. When you feel you are finished, thank Metatron for his presence and energy, snuff your candle, and go about your business.

Petition magick can be performed for any length of time. Depending on when it was begun, the situation may manifest by the end of a moon cycle, which is the general rule of thumb for this type of magick. For instance, if you want to draw a new career situation into your life, begin your petition magick on the first day of the waxing moon—the best energy for pulling something to you. If you want to release angry feelings about an ex-lover, begin your petition magick on the first day of the waning moon, the best energy for ridding yourself of what's unwanted. In many cases, the situation or item will manifest (or leave, if you're performing magick to release something) by the next moon phase to which it corresponds. If this is not the case, you might need to rethink your petition. Are you sure you are working with the best intentions? Is this really a good choice for you at this time? Meditation with Metatron might bring some answers to this puzzle.

One last word about magick: there is something to be said for acting in accordance. Metatron serves Creator, who created the Universe to run according to Natural Law. One Natural Law of the Universe is the Law of Attraction, or the idea that like attracts like. Work energy attracts work energy. Metatron is powerful, but nothing will substitute for hard work on your part as well. If you petition the Universe for a new job and ask for Metatron to lend his energy to this search, and then you do nothing to help yourself but sit in front of the television all day, it is highly unlikely that this wonderful new career opportunity is suddenly going to fall into your lap. When you work magick, you must also work in accordance, which means that you write up your resume, you send it out to online job sites, you make phone calls, and you go to job interviews. Miracles do happen, but your situation is going to manifest much quicker if you put energy into it every day. And every night, light your Metatron candle, read your petition aloud, and remember to believe that the magick is happening.

JEWELRY

I am a jewelry person, no question about it. I love the artistry of jewelry, and I enjoy finding and wearing pieces that reflect aspects of who I am. I find it ironic that, in my work as a massage therapist and healer, I can't wear rings, bracelets, or even long pendants while I work, because they interfere when I touch my clients. I do wear two pieces of jewelry every day, however: my wedding band and my protection necklace, a silver chain with two charms. One is a tiny pentacle that I bought for myself when I began serious pursuit of spiritual matters over seventeen years ago. The other is my guardian angel medallion. This charm reminds me of my constant connection to my personal guardian angel, and to the Archangels Michael (another of my favorites) and Metatron.

Like the tools already mentioned, you can charge an angel amulet to connect you with Metatron's energy. Many gift shops carry angel merchandise; some have lapel pins, charms for bracelets or pendants, and even smooth round chips with an angel image that can be carried in a coin purse or pocket. If you prefer a traditional medallion, you may have to find your local Roman Catholic boutique. These stores stock charms devoted to specific saints, among whom the Archangels Gabriel, Michael, and Raphael are usually included. I have not yet found any devoted to Metatron (or Uriel, for that matter), but you can purchase "generic" medallions depicting a simple guardian angel.

If these do not suit you, you may prefer to purchase prayer beads or malas from a store specializing in these items. Malas are used by devotees in Buddhism and Hinduism to count prayers, mantras, and/or prostrations. They are similar to the Catholic rosary, which offers a physical way to keep track of a set of prayers said by the spiritual student. Many malas are made with 111 beads, which connects them intricately to Metatron's energy and the power of the number eleven (see chapter 1). Whether you choose a prayer bracelet, an angel medallion, or a special stone ring to represent Metatron, you can empower your jewelry in the same way.

Take the chosen item to your special meditation space or your altar. If you have made a Metatron candle, light it. If not, light a white candle to symbolize connecting to Divine energies. If you have other items devoted to Metatron (a crystal, spray, or potpourri, for example), you may wish to put these out on your altar as well. Find a comfortable position and close your eyes while holding your jewelry in your hands. I like to place the piece in the palm of my left hand and then cup my right hand over it, completely covering it. Visualize the jewelry in your mind, and see it surrounded by white light. This light, the love energy of the Divine, completely encompasses your piece. Say to yourself, "This jewelry is completely bathed in the white light of the Divine and radiates that loving energy. The white light completely removes any negative or harmful energies that may be attached to this jewelry. These are released into the ethers to be transmuted into more positive energies."

See the white light fill the object until your piece of jewelry glows like a candle flame.

Still holding your jewelry, breathe in and call to Metatron in your mind. Invite him to come into your space. Use whatever words feel comfortable to you. Remember that he is a compassionate and loving being who only wishes to help you. If it helps you to connect with his energy, try chanting his name over and over. You will find as you chant that your energy starts to heighten and the chanting becomes faster and faster. This is an indication that the Archangel has drawn very close to you. The object you hold may begin to feel warmer in your hands. When this happens, stop chanting and say, "Archangel Metatron, thank you for your presence here. Please bless this jewelry with your wise, healing, loving energy. Help me to understand my connection to the Divine whenever I wear it.

Bring me peace and protection as a child of Creator, and know that I ask for nothing but positive and good energies to surround me and my life. Thank you for your intercession. Stay with me always and remind me of your presence. I welcome your help."

When you feel the object has been properly filled with the loving energy of the Divine, put it on, knowing that you will now always carry that energy with you whenever you wear it.

Dreamwork with Metatron

Our dreams can be a fascinating and fun way to connect with the world of spirit. In my work as a medium over the years, I have had the great fortune of accessing some of the other realms during my dreamtime, and I have met with my spirit guides as well as loved ones who have passed over. It is also possible to meet with angelic energies through dreamwork, and this is one way you may want to try to strengthen your connection to Metatron.

Before retiring for the night, try using the Healing Waters or Violet Wind meditation (see pages 46 and 52). Meditating with Metatron will help create a more peaceful state within you, and it will clear out any negative feelings or reservations you may have about connecting with the Archangel through your dreams. Put your Metatron crystal on your nightstand, or wear your Metatron jewelry to bed. As noted earlier, place your notebook next to the bed so that *as soon as you awaken,* you can write down whatever you remember.

Once you've meditated and placed your items nearby, take another moment to close your eyes. Say in your mind:

Metatron, please come to me in my dreams tonight.
Bring to me sacred messages that I need to know.
Help me to be the best person I can possibly be.
I await your presence in the world of dreams.

Know that by saying this, you have set your intention (to receive messages from Metatron in your dream state), and you have made it clear that you expect to receive these messages. Lie down and go to sleep.

When you awaken, no matter the time, allow yourself to become aware of your surroundings. Ask yourself, "What do I remember about my dream?" When images, feelings, colors, insights, and other recollections begin to flood into your head, take out your notebook and write them down. (It doesn't matter what your words look or sound like— scribble in the dark if you have to! Just get them down. If you are afraid you'll disturb your bed partner, try writing in the dark—or sleeping in another room for a few days. And be sure to take your notebook!)

Then put your notebook aside, close your eyes again, and thank Metatron for the symbols and messages he brought to you in your dream state. Go on back to sleep. If you wake up again during the night, repeat the process. Remember: you need not try to interpret the messages right away. Just write now, so you can analyze later.

When you have time the next day, take out your notebook and review what you wrote. The words and images may seem random, but remember that Metatron may speak to you through symbolism. Much of the information that comes from those dwelling in the etheric planes is conveyed this way. If you have a book on symbolism or dream interpretation, you might try using it—but keep in mind that your symbols reflect *your* beliefs and interpretations. Let's say, for example, that your favorite color is black, and last night you dreamed you were in a black room. When you awakened, you felt peaceful and rested. But when you open your dream interpretation book, it tells you that the color black symbolizes chaos or unrest. In instances with such conflicting views, you should go with your own feeling. If you like black, Metatron might be using the color to symbolize a positive feeling or quality. Perhaps he is trying to tell you that you need more quiet time by going "into the void," or that finding a peaceful solution to a problem or conflict is the best idea.

Take some time to look at all of your symbols together, too. They may seem to be unrelated, but often you can construct a pattern from strange objects when you look at their symbolic meanings. Perhaps you asked Metatron for insights concerning your job. When you woke up in the middle of the night, you remembered dreaming about a yellow bird in a cage, so you scribbled that in your notebook. You went back to sleep, and the next time you awakened, you recalled that your boss was in your dream, and she didn't look very happy. You jot this down as well before getting up to take your morning shower. Later in the morning, on your coffee break, you look at your notes. What could these symbols mean in relation to your job?

A few things pop right into my mind when I analyze the yellow, caged bird. The color yellow is often associated with intellect, knowledge, and wisdom. Birds or winged creatures can also represent our thought patterns and ideas. Isn't it interesting that both of these pertain to the realm of knowledge? The bird is also inside a cage, a definite symbol for boundaries, restrictions, and the removal of freedom. Putting this together, I would conclude that the image symbolizes a restriction of thought or ideas somehow connected to your job or career, since this is what you asked Metatron to comment on in your dream state.

You also dreamed later in the sleep cycle about your boss, who did not appear happy when you saw her. This could certainly be a precognitive vision, meaning that Metatron could be telling you in advance that your boss may be upset with you in the coming days. To determine this, you would have to monitor your boss's moods and reactions to you. Coupled with the first dream, it could mean that your boss is restricting you intellectually or creatively in this job, and that eventually, she will be unhappy with your work because you are unable to please her or because you don't know that you can.

Can you see how these symbolic interpretations can be pulled out of just two images that you had while sleeping? In this instance, Metatron gave some information that may be helpful to you in your job situation, and it is up to you to decide what you want to do with that information. Our dreams may give us a spiritual "heads-up"—which may help us avoid being blindsided and left reeling by something we didn't expect.

What if you set your intention at bedtime, go to sleep, and then wake up unable to remember any of your dreams? Keep trying! Some people normally dream more than others; some first need to work with Metatron on opening themselves up to angelic communication. Continue performing your angelic meditations as a keystone to accessing Metatron on a regular basis, and more than likely, your dream work will also begin to fill with visions. If you give up, you may never know what you could have achieved!

————————

We can build confidence in our connection to Creator and our own Higher Power by working with the Archangel Metatron, who dwells constantly in that divine energy. By working with Metatron in meditation and in dreams, and by creating tools to assist in connecting with his energy, we can reinforce our oneness with that divine energy and realize our full potential as co-creators with God.

THREE

Ceremony with Metatron

What is a ceremony? One dictionary defines it as "a formal act or set of acts established by custom or authority as proper to a special occasion, such as a wedding, religious rite, etc.," a rite being "any formal, customary observance, practice, or procedure."[1] In other words, a ceremony can be a formal way of experiencing a spiritual energy.

For those of us who grew up with or still participate in an organized religion, going to a house of worship is one way to experience ceremony. My entire family is Roman Catholic, and for at least the first eighteen years of my life, we attended Sunday Mass every week without exception. The Mass, the rite itself, is an experience that still reverberates deeply within me, if for no other reason than the

---

1 *Webster's New World Dictionary,* Third College Edition (New York: Simon & Schuster, 1988).

sheer repetition, my instant recognition of the prayers and the structure of its celebration. When my mother passed away, I took great comfort in her funeral Mass, in its familiarity and rhythm. There is something very soothing about finding a pattern and repeating it. It's a comfort all of us can appreciate whether we come from a religious background or not.

Whatever our cultual background, our lives probably include formal ceremonies of some kind: rituals or celebrations that mark significant milestones. High school and college graduations are marked by a commencement ceremony where the students march to accept their diplomas. Weddings are ceremonies that unite the lives of two people. All religions solemnize specific spiritual events with ceremonies—such as baptisms or christenings for children, in some traditions. We can also create and conduct our own ceremonies outside of the parameters of formalized religion to strengthen and grow as spiritual beings.

Connecting with the Archangel Metatron through ceremony can be deeply enriching and enlightening. With the Archangel's help, I have designed four rites to both further our relationship with him, and to help us in several specific areas: karma balancing, balancing masculine and feminine energies, balancing two worlds, and world healing. All four are outlined in this chapter. They can be performed once or many times, depending on your feeling and what you need to work on in your own journey. And all ceremony leads us back to the ultimate source of connection in life: to God, and our own inner divinity.

But first, try this balancing exercise. You can do it anytime you feel disconnected from your own spirit or out of sorts emotionally. The movements of this exercise, recommended by Metatron himself, can help you feel more centered and focused. Remember that the left side of the body is the receptive, "input" side, while the right side is the giving, "output" side. As you do this exercise, visualize both sides coming into balance. I like doing it in the morning so I can start the day with a fresh and focused perspective. It takes only a few moments, but its benefits last for many hours.

Metatron's Balancing Exercise

Stand with your arms at your sides and your feet planted shoulder-width apart, knees slightly bent. Inhale through your nose and lift your arms out to your sides in a fluid motion, palms up. Sweep your arms up in an arc until they are directly over your head, palms facing each other but not touching. Exhale through your mouth and lower your open right hand down in front of your body, with the open left hand following it closely, until both hands reach the middle of your chest, directly in front of your heart chakra. Inhale again and repeat the cycle: sweep your arms out to the sides and up in a fluid, circular motion, pausing with your palms facing each other above your head. Exhale, and this time lower your left hand first, followed closely by the right, until they reach the area of the heart chakra. Inhale and repeat again, but this time let the palms touch at the top of the arc. Exhale and bring them, still touching, down the front of your body, again stopping in front of the heart chakra. Inhale again, and enjoy the feeling of balance and peace you experience.

As you become more adept at this exercise, try expanding your breath awareness, synchronized with the motions. As your arms rise and your hands float above your head, concentrate on breathing in positive energy and balancing your own receptive energy. As you lower your hands, concentrate on releasing negative energy and transmuting it into a positive vibration. As your palms meet in the third cycle, know that you are a balanced individual who easily and lovingly both gives and receives.

Preparing for Ceremony

Before performing any of the ceremonies outlined here, take time to prepare and plan. Consider these steps:

1. *Choosing a ceremony space.* Most people who perform ceremony regularly like to create a dedicated sacred space. Rooms and other designated spaces hold energy. When you use the same ceremonial space every time, its energy vibration can be very beneficial to the rite's results. If your ceremony has no special requirements, a room that is quiet and feels good to you will be your best bet. I like to perform larger ceremonies in my dining room, smaller ones in my bedroom, near my altar. You may also consider choosing a space that suits the nature and purpose of each particular ceremony. If you'll be cooking as

a part of the ceremony, an obvious choice would be the kitchen. Bathrooms can be used for bathing or cleansing rituals. Don't discount the backyard, either. Outdoor ceremonies can connect us powerfully to the elemental and earth energies that reside in nature.

2. *Setting up an altar.* An altar is a special place reserved for the display and use of ritual items and other sacred tools. On my personal altar in my bedroom, I keep a variety of items depending on the time of year, my current spiritual work, and my mood. There is always a candle, which I light for prayer work. Other objects include special stones and crystals, pictures of passed loved ones, representations of Deity, messages from my spirit guides given through artwork or oracle cards, and the like. When I perform a special ceremony, I usually clear the altar and place objects that will be needed for the rite on it. You can create your own sacred altar in a special place in your home. Mine resides on a standing jewelry armoire. An altar can be as large or as small as you like. I have seen altars that are tiny corner tables and elaborate, multi-tiered cabinets. Even a shelf will suffice if space is limited. Whatever you choose, decorate your altar to honor your personal representations of the Divine (a statue of Buddha, a picture of Jesus, a ring of flowers for the Goddess). Everything needed for a ceremony can then be brought to your altar. If you don't have anywhere to

set up a permanent altar, you can create a temporary altar easily. Use your dining room table, a coffee or end table in the living room, or even a large piece of cardboard or wood covered with a tablecloth that rests on the floor of your basement. Remember: you are creating a sacred space, and the altar will be the focal point of it, where you will represent Divinity.

3. *Gathering tools.* In each of the ceremonies described here, I have listed any tools that you will want to include. Make sure you gather everything you need for your ceremony *before* you begin. A ceremony is all about focusing energy, which cannot be done if you are constantly leaving the ritual space to fetch a forgotten object. Once all of your tools are gathered, arrange them on the altar according to your own taste, preference, or tradition. Some folks may come from a magickal background and will want to honor the directions of certain energies. This is perfectly fine, but the ceremonies included here are meant to be accessible to all people regardless of training. Do what feels right to you. And don't forget this book (if you need it to follow the outline of the ceremony) as well as matches to light your candles!

4. *Preparing the mind and body.* The energy that we bring to a ceremony will directly affect anything we hope to create. This means that if we've planned a ceremony for 7:00 in the evening and then have a terrible time at work during the day, some time

should be spent clearing this negative energy away before beginning the ceremony. One way to help this is to take a ritual bath before beginning. Most people believe a bath is preferable to a shower, but either will suffice. Use bath salts or a shower gel that smells good to you and helps to elevate your mood. As you bathe, stay mindful and see yourself washing away any negative energy. Take a few moments to relax in the tub or under the shower spray, breathing deeply and filling yourself with positive and calm energy. When you emerge from the bath, you should feel better, more centered, and ready to begin your ceremony.

5. *Enjoying your ceremony.* Remember that ceremony is a way of connecting with Creator as well as the divine within ourselves. It is fine to be serious and to treat the act as sacred (because it truly is), but don't pressure yourself into trying to create the "perfect" rite. I have known many people who balk at doing their own ceremonies because they're afraid that they'll "do it wrong." If you light the candle at the wrong time in your ritual, who's going to know but you and God? And honestly, as a person who has been performing ceremonies for a long time, I've never noticed that God cares all that much. If you are approaching the rite with reverence and you end up knocking over the glass of water you've included, it's OK to laugh at yourself. Creator loves a sense of humor!

Now, with all of these tips in mind, read through the following ceremonies and see which one stands out to you. That may be the one you need most right now. Once you've seen how to perform the ceremony, you can look ahead at your calendar and plan when you might like to try doing it. Good luck, and know that Metatron will welcome the chance to help you connect more closely with Creator and to change the energy in your life for the better.

Balancing Karma with Metatron

One of my favorite expressions—one my friends and family have heard ad nauseam—is "Karma is an interesting thing." When I say this, I'm usually commenting on the fact that what goes around comes around, and that karma has made itself apparent because someone has gotten what he or she deserves.

One of the Natural Laws of the Universe, the Law of Karma, states simply that every cause has an effect. The important part of the Law of Karma is that we can always choose our action—we have free will at every moment of our lives. Even when our choices seem limited by circumstances, there is always a choice. In the instance of having only one path, we still have a choice: we can take the path, or we can remain where we are. Karma is not the same as the concept of fate; since we have free will, we can always change the direction our lives take. Fate implies that our lives are completely mapped out, and we're just along for the ride. Karma gives the concept of personal responsibility a whole other dimension, for we realize that we have true control over every aspect of our lives. See how very divine we truly are?

Many people also recognize in a discussion of karma the idea of past lives and reincarnation. Karma is often thought to be the repayment of past debts and sins. This notion, however, is far too simplistic, although it is true that we may carry karma from one lifetime into the next if we have not yet balanced it. Karma itself is not a negative thing, or a punishment meted out by the Universe to correct past mistakes. Karma, in and of itself, seeks only to balance energies.

Say, for example, that in a previous lifetime you owned a slave named Sue. In that lifetime, you treated Sue badly and never released her from her obligation to you. Now, fast-forward a few hundred years to the present. Sue is now your mother in this incarnation, and she has a very controlling personality. She phones you constantly to find out where you are and what you're doing. Her affection and concern are suffocating, but you can't find a way to tell her how her smother-love bothers you. Can you see how your mother's role in this lifetime may reflect a karmic imbalance that your two souls need to address? What choices could you make in this lifetime to help balance the karma between your soul and Sue's so that you no longer carry this karmic debt?

One thing that anyone can do is perform a ceremony to release karmic bonds and debts. Many times, forgiving your soul for wrongs done in previous incarnations can help balance karmic issues and break karmic behavior patterns. You don't need to be consciously aware of every karmic imprint you've made on every soul in the Universe, either. Performing a ceremony like this one can help alleviate these issues, and working with Metatron on them is a good place to start, since the Archangel has deep ties to healing karmic imbalances.

Karma Balancing Ceremony

What you'll need:
- a large bowl filled with spring water
- a white candle in a candle holder
- your Metatron candle in a holder
- a representation of your deity of choice
- matches or a lighter
- a candlesnuffer

When to perform this ceremony:
- on a Saturday
- on a new/dark moon
- during the autumn season
- or *all of these* for the most powerful results

Other optional items:
- decorate your altar in colors of black, silver, or white
- include dirt or sea salt to represent the element of earth, connected to releasing and forgiveness

Preparation: Make a forgiveness list. Take some quiet time to think about all the people in your life you need to forgive. Look back through your life; examine your childhood, your teen years, and your adult life up to now. Do not dwell on memories of hurt or pain; simply write a list of the people. Even if you don't think you can bring your-self to forgive a particular person who wronged you, write the name down anyway. Don't forget to include yourself: we often beat ourselves up for past mistakes. Take as much time as you need to complete your list.

At the time of the ceremony: Take your forgiveness list with you to your sacred space and get comfortable at your altar. Center yourself by breathing deeply and invite the Archangel into your space. Use your own words, or try these while lighting your Metatron candle:

> *Metatron, great and blessed angel of balance who serves only the Higher Power, I ask for your presence here today as I seek to balance my karmic debts. I realize that many in my life need forgiveness from me, and I am willing now to forgive them in my heart, mind, and soul. I, too, am in need of forgiveness, and I ask that as I forgive others, forgiveness flow to me as well. This forgiveness heals all karmic debts and energies, and as this forgiveness continues to flow, all karma comes into balance, as it is meant to be.*

Bring the bowl of water closer to you and say aloud, "I forgive _____," reading the name of the first person on your forgiveness list. As you speak the name, see any hurt or pain associated with this person leaving your body with your breath. Exhale it into the bowl of water and know that it is released from you.

Continue doing this exercise with every name on your list. Concentrate on forgiving each person and sending any negative energy away from you through your breath and into the water bowl. Know that as you breathe these names and declare your forgiveness, the waters begin to heal that energy. The Archangel Metatron, whom you invoked, stirs the vibration of karmic debt, bringing yours into balance with every breath you exhale.

When you have finished reading your entire list, say:

> *I now release one and all into the love and light of healing forgiveness. I am balanced and free of all debts, in this lifetime and in previous ones. I am whole and blessed.*

Light the white candle. See this candle as yourself and know that you burn brightly in the light of right thought and action.

Thank Metatron for his presence in whatever way feels comfortable to you. When you have finished, extinguish your Metatron candle, using your candlesnuffer.

Take the bowl of water outdoors and pour it onto the ground. As you do this, say:

> *This cleansing and healing water transmutes all negative energies deposited here. This water now nurtures and heals the earth. And so it is.*

(If you cannot water the ground outside, take your bowl into the bathroom and pour the water down the tub drain. You can say the same thing as you dispose of it.)

Return to your altar, and clear away anything that needs to be cleaned up. Let the candle burn for at least an hour after your ceremony, or burn it over the next several days until it is used up. (Anytime you leave the room or finish burning your candle, be sure to snuff it out so that you do not disperse the positive energy you have created.)

Balancing Masculine and Feminine Energies

The Natural Laws of the Universe have been created and instituted by God to govern the function of our vast cosmos. *The Kybalion: A Study of the Hermetic Philosophy of Ancient Egypt and Greece,* by Three Initiates, explores these in depth. As presented in this text, the Principle of Gender postulates that everything has masculine and feminine principles. Gender is not simply a state of being male or female; it reflects instead the manifestation of masculine and feminine energies on all planes of existence. Male or masculine energy is generally thought to be active, whereas female or feminine energy is passive or receptive. The active originates so that the receptive can create. This is the concept of yin (feminine) and yang (masculine) prominent in Eastern philosophies. If you look at the principles of yin and yang, you can see what appear to be opposites of nature:

Yin	Yang
passive	active
cold	hot
death	life
winter	summer
female	male
night	day
even	odd
moon	sun
water	fire

Within this philosophy, one property cannot exist without the other. In the Tai-ji shown here (the representation of the yin–yang circle), you can see that within each element resides a tiny piece of the other.

YANG   YIN

For nature to exist, these two opposites must depend upon each other. There is no better or worse, no right or wrong, contained in the Law of Gender. There is simply an acknowledgement that these properties exist because of one another, and they support each other in the fabric of the Universe. Between all of these elements is a flow that sustains the operation of the planes of existence. Spiritual nature is androgynous; when the yin and yang can be balanced, one understands intuitively how to act in all circumstances. Perhaps this is why Andrew Jackson Davis, a great trance channel of the nineteenth century, had this advice: "Under all circumstances, keep an even mind." [2]

We are, naturally, reflections of this same principle. Human beings possess both masculine and feminine attributes, as

2 Quoted in William Howitt, *The History of the Supernatural in All Ages and Nations* (Ann Arbor, University of Michigan Library, 2005), 226.

well as positive and negative traits. All of these qualities help to make a complete person. For example, aggression, a masculine energy, is often judged as a negative trait. However, someone who honors the aggressive part of his or her nature may be more balanced than a person who does not. Some non-aggressive folks bury these feelings deep within themselves because they were taught that aggression is a bad thing. Most, however, eventually must deal with a situation where this pent-up aggression rises to the surface, usually in an explosive manner. Would it be better to channel that energy in a more positive direction before it makes a violent appearance? Most likely it would.

We may also tamp down feelings if we've been taught that displaying them is inappropriate. Many people disconnect from their emotions because they believe, for whatever reason, that showing them is a sign of weakness. Emotional reactions are generally associated with the realm of feminine, or passive, qualities, and, especially in Western society, these traits are not usually viewed as desirable. We tend to value logical thinking, reason, and indifference over intuition, emotion, and passion. A well-balanced person, however, understands the importance of expressing emotion, both for one's own betterment and for the benefit of others.

These are only two examples of how balancing the Law of Gender, or the masculine and feminine energies within, can help us to become better people physically, emotionally, and spiritually. Performing a ceremony with Metatron with these concepts in mind can be an extremely powerful experience.

Masculine-Feminine Balancing Ceremony

What you'll need:

- a black pillar candle at least three inches thick

- a white candle of the same size

- a glass or aluminum pie plate

- thin black ribbon about twelve inches long

- thin white ribbon of the same length

- a long nail or ritual carving object (an athame or dagger, for example)

- your Metatron candle

- a representation of Deity

- a lighter or matches

- a candlesnuffer

When to perform this ceremony:

- on a Monday

- on a waxing or full moon

- during the spring season

- or *all of these* for the most powerful results

Other optional items:

- altar decorations in black, white, or silver

- moonstone, which can help balance emotional energy

- a small bowl of water to represent elemental energy associated with emotional balance

Preparation: When setting up your altar, place the white and the black pillar candles together in the pie plate. Set the ribbons and the carving tool nearby so that they are easy to reach during the ritual.

Take some time to examine your emotional landscape and to take stock of your masculine and feminine qualities. Which traits seem to be most prevalent in your life? Where do you seem to be lacking? Look at the list here and write down those that seem to fit your personality.

aggressive	*forgiving*	*reliable*
assertive	*friendly*	*removed*
bossy	*idealistic*	*sensible*
careful	*inflexible*	*serious*
caring	*introspective*	*silly*
compassionate	*involved*	*speculative*
critical	*judgmental*	*spontaneous*
devoted	*lenient*	*stubborn*
empathic	*logical*	*sympathetic*
extroverted	*passive*	*thick-skinned*
fact-oriented	*practical*	*thin-skinned*
fanciful	*realistic*	*unbending*
firm	*reasonable*	*whimsical*

Then try classifying each trait on your list as either masculine or feminine and count up each category. Are you more masculine or feminine in your energies? Remember, this has nothing to do with your gender. It has more to do with your emotions and how you deal with conflicts, obstacles, and growth opportunities.

Reflect on the areas of your life in which you can most clearly see the imbalance of masculine and feminine energies. What specific problems or obstacles have you encountered where you were either helped or hurt by being more masculine than feminine, or more feminine than masculine? In what current life situations might balancing these energies benefit you and produce a better outcome? Write these down, too, taking as much time as you need. Try to release any judgments about yourself as you make your list.

At the time of the ceremony: Take your list with you to your ceremony space and get comfortable at your altar. Inhale and exhale deeply to center and focus yourself. Light the Metatron candle on your altar and invoke the Archangel, telling him why you are connecting with him. Try these words if none come to you:

> *Archangel Metatron, great angel of the Highest and servant of Creator, I ask for your presence and power here today. I seek balance within myself: the balance of masculine and feminine, light and dark, active and passive, positive and negative. I know that each of these cannot exist without the other, and so I ask for your intercession in bringing my nature and energy into harmony and equilibrium with the great I Am that is within and without the whole of the Universe.*

Address any specific situations you wrote down by saying:

> *Metatron, I seek balance for myself especially in the following situations:*

Read what you have written aloud, or describe to Metatron what is happening in your own words. There is no rush; simply say how you feel and what has transpired. Recall that there is no judgment in this process.

When you've finished, say:

> *I release the feelings I have toward these situations and know that I now bring peace and balance to them through the equilibrium that is achieved within myself.*

Take the white candle and hold it in your hands. This candle represents the masculine energies within your being. Concentrate on this as you take your carving tool and write the word "masculine" on the candle. Take your time, and focus on the attributes you listed on your paper as male energies. Then place the white candle in the pie plate and pick up the black candle, which represents the feminine energies within you. Focus on these energies and the words you wrote to describe them as you carve the word "feminine" on the candle. When you are finished, place it back into the pie plate.

Now take the black ribbon and tie one end around the middle of the white candle. Tie the white ribbon around the middle of the black candle. Now take the two loose ends and tie them together, black and white, linking the two candles. Place the candles as far apart as possible within the confines of the pie plate, tautening the ribbons.

Now visualize peace, harmony, and balance coming to your life and the situations you have written about on your paper. See yourself as a whole and balanced person. Know that you are in equilibrium as you light the white candle and say:

I honor the masculine side of myself.

Light the black candle and say:

I honor the feminine side of myself.

Touch both candles at the same time using both hands and say:

I honor the whole of Creator within me. I honor the masculine, the active, the positive, the light. I honor the feminine, the passive, the negative, the dark. I am whole and balanced, and I bring these energies to every person and situation in my life. And so it is!

Thank Metatron for his presence and help in your ceremony by saying:

Gracious and loving Metatron, I thank you for your help here. Stay if you will, go if you must. Hail and farewell.

Snuff out your Metatron candle.

Allow the candles to burn in the pie plate for as long as you can. If you must put them out, use your snuffer. You may also relight them when you have time to let them burn. As they diminish, they will leave wax in the bottom of the plate, blending the two colors, with the ribbons becoming part of this mixture. When they have completely burned out, allow the wax to harden. You can then break it apart and carry a piece of it with you in a purse or pocket to remind you of the balance created in your ritual. If the wax clings to the pie plate, place it in the freezer for a few hours. It should pop right out. You can bury the rest of the wax in your yard. Never throw candle wax away immediately, for it contains the energy you have sought in your ritual. But you can deprogram the energy by holding your hands over the wax and saying:

> *I release from this substance all ritual energies infused within it. These energies transmute into the Light and are now neutralized from this matter. So be it.*

Once this is done, it is safe to throw the candle wax away. You may also deprogram the energy and save the wax to make your own candles, removing any ribbon from the wax. Books on candlemaking are easily found.

Standing in Two Worlds

If you have been a spiritual student for any length of time, I'm sure you have encountered frustration trying to balance the mundane world with your spiritual studies. When I first began studying mediumship at a formal institution in 1996, I had to take weeklong classes to obtain my credentials. This was difficult: I had two babies at home who needed attention, and the drive to class took about three hours. I had to make sacrifices to concentrate on this work, and the people close to me sacrificed as well. Thoughts of balancing my mundane life and my spiritual pursuits were always on my mind.

Not much has changed for me since then, even though I have obtained the credentials I originally sought (and a few more). I am a perpetual student, and I believe in continuing to study in order to grow as much as I possibly can. It's always a struggle to figure out how much time and energy I can give to my spiritual work without sacrificing too much time with family, friends, church members, clients, and other people in my life. Burning the proverbial candle at both ends is nothing new to me; it is, however, something I tire of often, because it seems to be a constant battle.

I believe, however, that the Universe is a place of balance, and the natural condition of the Universe *is* balance. Therefore, it stands to reason that if we feel out of balance or overstretched, especially in the area of the spiritual versus the mundane, we can correct this condition, either through our own actions or by asking for help from the higher planes of existence. This is where Metatron can help us through ceremony.

Balancing Two Worlds Ceremony

What you'll need:
- a deck of playing cards
- your Metatron candle
- a representation of Deity
- a lighter or matches
- a candlesnuffer

When to perform this ceremony:

- on a Wednesday

- on a full moon

- during the summer season

- during an "in-between" time, like dusk or dawn

- or *all of these* for the most powerful results

Other optional items:

- altar decorations in gray, silver, or orange

- carnelian or opal gemstones, which can attract wisdom and clarity in all matters

Preparation: For this ceremony, you will need a *sturdy* table. If your altar is stable and large enough, you might choose to use it. If so, do *not* cover it with a cloth. You may still dress it up with your statue of deity and your Metatron candle, but you need to have a decent amount of uncovered space for the ceremony task. If your altar is not large enough, you may want to work at a kitchen or dining room table, or set up a card table near your altar.

Take some time to reflect upon how your spiritual life currently fits into your mundane life. Do you feel you are neglecting one for the other? If you need more prayer or meditation time, how might it fit into your schedule? Do you hear complaints from your partner or children because you are always at a yoga class or reading esoteric books? Really think about what you would like to see happen in your life in this regard. Remember that even if you cannot see a viable solution, the Universe can create one because the Universe is all about balance, and everything is possible.

At the time of the ceremony: Go to your ceremony space and light your Metatron candle. Invoke his energy by saying:

> *Archangel Metatron, I ask you to be with me now. You have dwelled in two worlds—this physical world and in the spiritual planes. It is my fervent wish to be closer to Creator, and yet I must also live and work in this world. Help me find the perfect balance between these two so that I may easily move in both spheres, never neglecting one for the other, and satisfying my own deep yearning for knowledge and growth.*

Close your eyes and breathe deeply, finding the still point within where you feel relaxed and centered. When you have reached this state, open your eyes and take out your deck of playing cards. Begin building a house with them, one by one. As you build, repeat the following affirmation out loud:

> *I easily balance my spiritual growth with my mundane life. All is in perfect balance, and I am happy and fulfilled.*

If your house of cards falls, do not give up. Stay focused, relaxed, and positive. Continue building and reaffirming your statement until you have managed to make a three-story house of cards. Know that the Archangel Metatron will help you throughout this process.

Then take your house apart and put the cards away. Thank Metatron for his presence and assistance:

> *Archangel Metatron, I thank you for being with me and for guiding me to a more balanced state, both in this world and in the spirit planes. Help me to maintain this equilibrium as I continue to seek spiritual knowledge and as I enjoy the pleasures and challenges of the physical realm. Hail and farewell.*

Snuff out your Metatron candle and clear your sacred space.

World Issues

It is no great surprise to anyone living in our world today that our challenges are tremendous. Disease, war, poverty, hunger, oppression—these terrible situations have plagued society for thousands of years, and they will continue to challenge us all as we go forward. For many people, these issues create a sense of outrage, anger, hurt, sadness, or other feelings that can sometimes overwhelm, especially for people who are very sensitive and empathic to the energies present. It presents to us a daunting spiritual challenge: how do we reconcile these problems with our belief in a loving, nurturing Divine Presence and an ordered Universe?

Many of these problems have been attracted into the physical plane because of our human resistance to letting change happen. The Natural Law of Attraction states that like attracts like. We may not believe that we are asking for disease and poverty and war to run rampant throughout humanity, and yet we watch violent films for entertainment. We try to hide the spiritual and emotional voids we carry at a soul level, opening our physical bodies to manifestations of these problems as ulcers, headaches, or more severe chronic and acute conditions. We nourish ourselves with material things instead of allowing our spiritual connections and the Divine Presence to fulfill us. And when we see instances of cruel and abject poverty and disease, we feel helpless, thinking, "What can I do? I can't even care for those closest to me."

Creator and His messenger, Metatron, understand our fear and uncertainty, yet both want us to feel more in control and less fearful of the problems in our modern world. There are many wonders to behold, and God certainly wants us to concentrate on these. He also wants us to understand our role as co-creators of the Universe, and to use the awesome power that He bestows upon us to bring more balance and peace to the world. To this end, Creator sends Metatron, the Voice of God and the Angel of the Presence, to school us in how to achieve these ends.

World Healing Ceremony

What you'll need:

- a newly purchased small houseplant

- your Metatron candle

- a representation of Deity

- matches or a lighter

- a candlesnuffer

When to perform this ceremony:

- on a Sunday

- on a new moon

- during the spring season

- or *all of these* for the most powerful results

Other optional items:

- altar decorations in gold and green, to honor illumination and healing

- a clear quartz crystal charged to heal the earth

- paints or markers

Preparation: This ceremony focuses healing energy for all areas of the earth. This is a broad idea that includes bringing peace, prosperity, and universal love to all communities on the planet. Do not feel overwhelmed or daunted by the large-scale nature of this intention. Metatron's energy is vast and can illuminate any and all dark areas and dispel thoughts of defeat. Keep a positive and productive attitude as you prepare for this ritual. See in your mind the healing of the earth as if it has already taken place. Feel peace within your own self and allow it to radiate out of you as you dress your altar and gather your ceremony tools.

Purchase a small houseplant for this ceremony. Choose one that is easy to care for, especially if you know you don't have an especially green thumb. Some good choices include spider plants, jade plants, Christmas and Easter cacti, and aloe plants. First check the information included with the plant to see if it will fit into your home environment: for example, if your house doesn't get much sun, don't choose a plant like jade that enjoys bright light.

As you travel home with your plant, take a few moments to welcome its energy. This may sound silly, but plants are living things and thus respond to thought energies, just as other creatures do. In your ceremony, your plant will represent the entire planet, so you may even want to name it Earth or Gaia. If you are crafty, you might decorate your plant's pot with markers or paints, labeling it with its new name or drawing a picture of the planet Earth on it. Keep it fun and relaxing, and remember as you paint that you are sending healing and love to the earth, and your new plant represents the way this positive energy will grow in the future.

At the time of the ceremony: Go to your altar and place your new plant in the center of it. Get comfortable and light your Metatron candle. Invoke Metatron's energy by calling him in with your own words, or say:

Archangel Metatron, friend and guardian of humanity and our planet Earth, be with me now as I work today. Our planet is in need of many things: healing for the soil, for the water, and for the air; love, unity, and peace between its peoples; prosperity and stewardship for all of its creatures to thrive. I ask this day for you to join your power with mine as I concentrate on creating this healing energy for all who dwell on the planet Earth, and for the highest and the best to come to every corner of the planet.

Cup your hands around the plant's pot. Close your eyes and breathe deeply, centering and balancing yourself. When you feel that sense of equilibrium, bring your attention to your plant. Can you feel its energy? Lift your hands from the pot and bring them around the leaves of the plant, holding them about a half an inch away. Do you sense any heat or any subtle pulsations from the plant? All living things exude energy, and most people can feel an aura as heat or cold, tingling, throbbing, and other various sensations. If you can't feel the plant's energy, don't worry about it. Simply know that it is there, and that you can affect the plant's energy by sending your own positive thoughts toward its auric field.

As you hold your hands above the plant, visualize that you are holding the entire planet Earth between your palms, sending love and healing energy to it through your hands. See this healing flow from your hands as waves of golden or white light. Imagine this as vividly as you can. Hold the thought in your mind and heart that the plant represents the planet Earth, and that you are sending healing and love to the entire globe. Now add to your visualization a picture of the Archangel Metatron. See his hands on top of yours; imagine him adding his powerful energy. See him sending healing and light to the planet as you channel this loving energy. Know in your heart that by visualizing this, it *is* happening, and you *are* aiding the planet with Metatron's help. Repeat in your mind, "I am healing the planet Earth. I send love and help to all who need it. This channeled love and healing energy make a difference in the life of every creature and system within our planet. And so it is."

Continue to build the power of this healing. You might chant a phrase such as "healing and love, healing and love," over and over, faster and louder each time, until you feel you can no longer contain the energy. Then, in your visualization, release it in a wave over the planet Earth and see the energy entirely encompassing the globe. Say aloud, "This healing is done. And so it is!"

If you have included a quartz crystal for your ceremony, take it now and hold it between your hands. Infuse it with healing energy, charging it to bring peace, love, and blessings to the Earth. Dig a small hole in the plant's dirt and place the crystal within it. Cover it up and know that the crystal will continuously emit healing energy to both the plant and to the planet that it represents.

Thank Metatron for his important contribution to your ceremony. Dismiss him respectfully and clear your altar space. Place your plant in an appropriate spot in your home. Whenever you water it or clean around it, remember to say a special prayer and send more healing energy to the planet, invoking Metatron's energy when doing so. He will be happy to lend his help at any time.

———

Performing a ceremony is a beautiful, meaningful way to connect with our inner divinity and reach higher in our consciousness. Using ceremony to communicate with Metatron and to entreat him for help on particular issues can bring anyone a powerful sense of oneness with the whole of creation. If you have enjoyed working on these ceremonies with Metatron, perhaps you will be inspired to create some of your own rites. These rituals can be planned and executed anytime you seek a rich spiritual experience that will resonate afterward for many days to come.

FOUR

*M*etatron Speaks

As a professional medium, I find myself speaking to spirits, angels, and other nonphysical beings quite often. By definition, a medium is someone who is sensitive to the vibrations of the spirit world and can communicate with entities there.[1] With my clients and students, I spend many working hours listening to and relaying messages from passed-over loved ones, spirit guides and teachers, and angels. Usually when I am doing a reading or teaching a class, Spirit and the angels use mental mediumship to convey their messages. This means that the messages I impart to those listening come through my internal senses of clairvoyance (clear seeing), clairaudience (clear hearing), clairsentience (clear feeling), or claircognizance (clear understanding). I then verbally pass those messages on to whomever they are meant for, and my job as a medium, or intermediary, is done. There are,

---

1 For more on this subject, see my 2006 book *So You Want to Be a Medium? A Down-to-Earth Guide* (Woodbury, MN: Llewellyn).

however, other methods by which Spirit and the angels can communicate to those here in the physical world.

Channeling is one of these methods. As a channel, a person achieves a different state of consciousness, called trance, by which he is able to release his own personality for a short amount of time to allow another entity (a spirit guide, angel, or other evolved being) to inhabit his body and speak through him. Think of this definition of the word "channel," provided by *Webster's New World Dictionary*: "a course through which something moves or is transmitted, conveyed, or expressed." I like this because it conjures a specific picture, implying a waterway. Visualize a stream or a brook running through a forest. See the water flowing over the stones and rocks within its banks. Those banks and the riverbed are the channel through which the water flows. Channeling a spirit is no different. The person who is channeling is the conduit through which the identity, the energy, the essence, of a particular spiritual entity passes. While that entity—guide, deceased person, or angel—is within the channel, his or her energy speaks, writes, or otherwise communicates using the body, mind, and voice of the channeler. When the communication is over, the entity departs from the channeler's body, and the channeler's own spirit retakes control.

To some people, channeling is a more accurate means of spirit communication, because the channel or medium's own mind is taken out of the equation, leaving the entity to communicate directly to those who wish to be a part of that process. Despite our efforts, mediums sometimes color a message when it is delivered. The entity communicating can only use the medium's mind to convey its thoughts, feelings, and advice. The medium may inadvertently add to or subtract from the meaning of the message simply because the process itself is not perfect. When a medium channels, however, the entity gets to communicate its message directly to its audience, no matter how large or how small.

Although this may sound exciting and enthralling, channeling can be a long and arduous process to undertake and master. I believe all students can be taught how to induce a trance and how to allow positive energies to channel messages through them, just as I believe all of us can learn how to tap into our mediumship potential to speak directly to Spirit and the angels. I do not, however, believe that channeling can be taught through the pages of a book. In order to channel safely, I highly recommend finding a physical teacher who can instruct you in the mechanics of trance work.

There is, however, a simpler practice, somewhat similar to channeling, that can be incorporated in the work we are doing in this book with Metatron. Let's discuss inspirational writing, a wonderful method to employ in communicating with the Archangel.

Inspirational Writing

Inspirational writing is a form of channeling that does not require a great deal of training or practice. Nor does the medium or channel have to lose complete control of his or her consciousness to allow the spirit entity to communicate.

One of the best examples of inspirational writing we have in the Western world is the Bible. I believe that the Bible was divinely inspired. Did Creator actually channel through the men who wrote the various sections of the Bible? I don't think so, but I do believe that Creator inspired them to write the words they did. I believe, for example, that the apostle Paul had some trouble with the early Christians in various regions, and he wanted to help them. He asked for God's guidance, and he felt compelled, in one instance, to sit down and write a letter to the Corinthians. Does this mean that everything in that letter is exactly as God intended it to be? No, probably not, because those ideas have filtered through Paul's own mind before being put to paper. But nor does it mean that Paul was unconnected with Divinity when he wrote that letter. As long as he set his intention to connect with God and to write something helpful to the Corinthians, then his letter is an example of inspirational writing.

Now, I'm not claiming here to have some insight into the mind of Paul, or into God's own mind, for that matter. I am assuming something here, and it is a big assumption. I am assuming that Paul did indeed sit down to write that letter to the Corinthians with the intention of bringing them wisdom and love from God. This *must* be your intention any time you hope to participate in the process of inspirational writing. It is not something to play around with, like a parlor trick or a game. It is a valid way of connecting to divine energy, and it must be treated with respect. And honestly, the more respect you give to the process, the better your results will be.

You can use inspirational writing to connect with any of your spirit guides or angels. The Archangel Metatron is no exception. As you can see from the examples in this book, Metatron is more than willing to connect with you and to give you insight into all kinds of topics. I also found that he is open to communicating in this way about personal issues as well as global ones. I have not included my personal correspondences here, but Metatron is always able to help with matters large and small.

If you would like to try doing some inspirational writing with Metatron, find a time when you won't be disturbed. If you can write in your meditation space or on your altar, even better, but you may prefer to find a spot where you can write at a table. I find this better than trying to balance a pad of paper in my lap. Whatever you decide, bring your Metatron candle with you or keep your Metatron crystal or other tool nearby so you can feel his energy this way as well: it will improve your focus as you begin. You may wish to play some quiet music, too.

When you are ready to start, sit comfortably and close your eyes. Find the stillness within yourself that you discover when you meditate. Concentrate on your breathing and allow yourself to relax and focus. Visualize yourself surrounded by a ring of white light—the energy of Creator, in which no harmful or negative energy or entity can dwell. Repeat this thought in your mind and know without a doubt that as you stand between the worlds, you stand in the light of God. Let this sense of calm and peace penetrate you, and then call to Metatron in your mind. Know that when you invoke him, he comes immediately, and you feel his presence with you.

Once you connect in this way, tell Metatron that you wish to speak to him through inspirational writing. Ask him to inspire your thoughts with his own so that you can record anything he wishes to impart to you. Focus on working with only the highest and the best intentions, and pick up your pen. Clear your mind, and allow Metatron to inspire you. What words begin to form? What images come into your head? Write them down. Don't stop to make sure your spelling is correct or even that your sentences make sense. The grammar is not important; the message is. Keep writing until the idea or notion seems to dry up. This may indicate that the line of thought is finished. Another different topic may then begin, or it may simply signal the end of the correspondence.

If you need a specific question answered, write it at the top of a clean sheet of paper. Concentrate on this matter and ask that all answers pertain to this question. Let Metatron inspire you to jot down any and all words connected to this issue, even if they don't make complete sense. When you have finished your writing, ask Metatron to stay with you as you piece together the words. Allow him to guide you further as you look for meanings and connections within the correspondence. Often, the answer will snap into place as you read through the jumble of words—you'll see how they're all connected and how they point to an answer to your dilemma.

To finish this section, I asked Metatron to say anything else he wished to convey to his audience. The following piece of inspirational writing will, I hope, convince you of Metatron's very loving, very accessible energy.

It is a great honor to be able to speak to you. I AM Metatron, and I AM always. There is no beginning and no ending. This is a great truth that you should know, because so many of you worry about where you came from and where you are going. You came from God, and you go to God. There is nothing else. All is God, and all is good.

I asked this one to be my channel at this time for a purpose. You are all called to this higher purpose. If you are reading this, this is your calling, and God asks you to heed it. You are called to be all that you are, and you are God incarnate. Some think only certain souls have this connection, this divine nature. I tell you, it is within each of you. You are all divine, as Jesus is, as Buddha is, as so many of the human masters are. You have not embraced your own divinity, and so you suffer in this lifetime. When you are able to embrace that divinity, you will no longer suffer, because you will no longer doubt.

You will understand the deep connection to God that is within you, and you will constantly strive to honor it. You will comprehend your own power. It is not power in the sense of evil or greed, which is what so many associate with the word. It is power to love, and this is the strongest force in the Universe. Once you learn how to use this power, nothing on your physical plane of existence will ever be the same. Those great human masters, Jesus and the rest, tried to teach you how to use this power. The answers are all there. I AM here to help you understand this as well. Ask me, and I will serve you as best I can.

Never doubt that I AM here. I AM within you, and I help connect you to God. I AM without you, and I help you connect to your brothers and sisters on the earth plane. This is my great privilege and my great task. I have been in shadows for many years, because people did not understand the nature of angels. Do not rely upon me, for it is your task to become who you are meant to be, to step into your own divinity. But do know that I can help you realize your potential. I AM Metatron, Voice of God. Hear this now, beloved of God.

Words of Wisdom from Metatron

As I became more comfortable with the process of inspirational writing with Metatron, I found myself concentrating on certain issues and problems facing the world. As a spiritual student, I often contemplate how our actions ripple out from us, like rings from a pebble in water, affecting others around us in ways both large and small. I realized that these thoughts and questions were often on my mind as I sat down to commune and write with Metatron, and many of his responses came at times when I needed answers about certain subjects. On the next few pages, you will read Metatron's comments on several topics. I hope you'll enjoy the correspondence as much as I enjoyed the process.

ON THE NATURE OF ANGELS AND FALLEN ANGELS

I AM here. I AM always here. You ask about the nature of angels. Angels have always been, just as human beings have always been and will continue on at the time of death. Death is just a change in the energy vibration. Angels do not die, for we are naught but energy; we dwell in God's constant vibration and can move swiftly from one plane of energy to another. This is why we are often depicted with wings. Wings and halos. We are not holier than you! We just have very powerful auras, energy bodies that surround us. We do not have bodies as humans do. We can assume a body if it is needed, but angelic incarnation is rare, as we have discussed. Angels have always been one with the God nature, just as you are one with Him. Angels are bound to God and are bound to do His will. We dwell always in God's presence, for He dwells always at the forefront of our thoughts. It is when an angel acts without putting God first in those thoughts that the angel may "fall from grace," as you call it. Angels are always able to go back to God's energy, just as humans are. Some angels choose to dwell forever in those dark thoughts. And so they fall, as you say. They do not return to God, and they dwell in sorrow. Some may then torment other creatures, because they are separated from God. God does not prevent this because they can always return to God. There is nothing preventing their return but their own choice. It is the same with you. God's forgiveness is everlasting and abundant. Never forget this, beloved of God.

ON THE PLANES OF THE UNIVERSE

Every person is in the process of becoming what he or she needs to be. I AM here to help you in that process. All energies move toward becoming one again with the Divine Source, God, in the Universe. The Universe is more complex than you know; there are many worlds, many planes that you will not explore in this lifetime—not because they are closed to you, but simply because you are working toward other goals and ends and will not have the time to explore them. This is why there are infinite lifetimes and infinite expressions of life within the Universe, and why some of those expressions may never know the vastness of the other lives around them. You are souls journeying. The afterlife is a continuation of this journey. Souls that speak from other planes of existence sometimes talk of seeing other realms beyond what humans call the afterlife. This is because the soul is freed from narrow thinking upon the death of the body, if the soul chooses this, and can move freely from plane to plane, seeing other worlds and experiencing other realms. In the body, humans can do this through meditation, out-of-body traveling, and dreams. Many, however, doubt the reality of these experiences because they say they cannot be proven. I say, trust what God shows to you, for these experiences are real, and they are Divine.

Many ask about meditation. Why is it so difficult? Beloved, you make it difficult through your own negative thoughts and feelings about it. The human mind is like a minefield that your soldiers create for the enemy. You are not your own enemy—why do you sabotage your own progress by doubting the process? What you experience in your meditations is real. Trust it. Yes, it is a matter of learning to calm your mind and body so you can focus and concentrate. This can be learned. You must train yourself to do this if you hope to achieve enlightenment, and especially if you seek peace in this lifetime. There is no other road to peace in the human world on Earth but through the attainment of peace within oneself.

ON ANGELS' AVAILABILITY TO HUMANITY

The angels are sometimes saddened because so many human beings do not recognize our appearances and the love we send to you every day. It is our nature to love, and we can do nothing that is not in the love vibration. Please know that we surround you always and have your best interests at the forefronts of our minds, along with our devotion to God. Ask us for help and guidance. You need not ask aloud. We can and do hear your thoughts, prayers, and petitions. How can you think for an instant that God does not hear your prayers? Through our energy, your needs are channeled directly to Him, and He instructs us through our own nature in the best way to help you. Trust that we will lead you in the right direction. When your heart fills with love and warmth, you will know you are in the right place or have made the correct decision. Doubt feels cold and isolating. This is not the feeling you should have if your decision is in line with God's nature. So many of you ask for our intercession and then cannot or do not recognize our influences when we make them. If you need help recognizing our messages, ask for that, too. We want to be of service; it is our primary purpose, and fulfilling it brings us to that warm, loving energy that feeds our connection to God. Allow us into your life. Know without a shadow of doubt that we exist.

ON HUMANITY'S NEED FOR PEACE

There is great sadness and unrest in your world today because so many have moved themselves away from thoughts of God and into thoughts of ego. Some claim to be close to God, even working for God, but acts of violence, war, and greed are never acts of God. No one religion or group owns the path to enlightenment. To think so only shows the nature of humanity and its attachment to ego. Ego is not entirely a detriment; it keeps you focused on important matters such as survival and commitment to work. It does, however, sometimes scare you into thinking that you need particular things, material and otherwise, to make you happy or fulfill you in this lifetime. Beloved, you need nothing in this lifetime but your connection to God. We angels understand that the world in which you live is filled with distractions, obstacles, challenges . . . many ideas, philosophies, worries, and the like that demand your attention and turn you away from keeping God foremost in your thoughts. Angels do not have these same distractions, but we can become preoccupied, as you do, which is why we understand. When you have trouble choosing a path, ask yourself which way will bring you closer to God, to your Higher Nature.

Ask which choice is filled with love and compassion, and which choice better serves the All, rather than only serving you or those close to you. This question usually helps reveal the path where you can walk in God's footsteps. We understand that this is not always easy, and often this path is the hardest to follow. That is why we are here to help you—call on us!

Many people ask why there is no peace in the world. There will never be peace until all humanity can stop putting ego first and start putting God first instead. Do not feel that this is impossible—it is not! Everything is possible with God! But people must be taught from infancy that every energy in the Universe is connected, and that what hurts one energy, one creature, one person, hurts the entire fabric of the Universe. When one suffers, all suffer. Many people cannot see this, not until they can tune into these subtle energies and feel the pain that ripples along the web that connects all together. Children understand this, and yet most adults say they are more self-centered. This is because children do not question their place in the fabric of the Universe. They understand on an intrinsic level that God loves them, and that the Universe is a place of love and compassion. Only as they get older do they begin to fear and to question, which changes the way they view the world. Humanity needs to return to a simpler mindset to move closer to God. Thinking more simply does not mean you are stupid or ignorant. Thinking more simply means connecting all thoughts to love, which is the heart of God, and thus rendering all actions outside of love impossible to carry out. This is when peace will be achieved—when all humanity can act in constant synergy with the love energy that is the core of the Universe.

Of course you should pray for peace. Always ask for that which is needed, for God hears all these prayers. But always ask, too, that your own aura and energy of love be strengthened so that you can begin to be a source of peace to others. When one emanates peace, the others around cannot help but feel it. Sometimes, those around you may seem jealous or upset and hurl negative energy or attitudes at you. This is a challenge to keep your love energy high. Remember that they only do so out of fear. What people do not understand frightens them. In time, they will learn more about this energy themselves, and they will see the value of keeping their own love energy as high as possible. Until then, be an example to them of the potential to love—a potential possessed by every human being.

ON LAUGHTER AND HUMOR

In the midst of this communication, where so many subjects seem serious, it is important to keep a sense of humor and lightheartedness. Remember that God is love, and that laughter is essential to happiness. Humanity is closest to God in moments of humor, especially gentle, loving humor. Crass or grotesque humor serves a purpose at some times, but innocent laughter is infinitely more appealing. Look at a child when she laughs. The smallest, most insubstantial things bring smiles to a child. This is because of her simplicity. Some of the hardest lessons in life would become considerably easier to learn if humanity could approach them from a child-like perspective, a simpler view. Children remember that play and laughter are essential to their being. Adults seem to forget this and make no time for what they consider to be frivolous activities. This echoes our lesson of balance: you cannot have work without play, darkness without light, sorrow without happiness. Take time to enjoy; smile and laugh. It is an essential part of being human, and when a person laughs, God does, too.

ON THE NATURE OF EVIL

What is evil but the absence of love? Everything that separates us from God is that which is not love, and is therefore evil in its essence. "Evil" is a strong word that brings fear to most humans, but it is not something to fear. Evil will always be present because you cannot have love without it. It is the opposite of love, the opposite of good, the opposite of positive. It is a Universal Law: all must be balanced, and the presence of evil brings balance to this equation. You cannot have one without the other. But humanity should not fear this evil, for its presence does not give it power. Only acting upon its presence brings it the power to harm. Lurking within the heart of every person is the potential for evil, because you cannot be human without it. It is there, but it is not something to fear, for you can always choose love over evil. This is free will, the great gift God bestows upon every human creature, and exercising this free will and choosing to live in love is humanity's greatest challenge. The choice to do something easier, something that may not seem evil but that does not come from a place of love, may tempt a person, and it is in these moments that God calls you to put aside the easy task and dig deep within your being to find the strength to choose the harder one, the action that is filled with love. It is when evil is chosen out of laziness, out of grief, out of lack of compassion, that it begins to look as if evil is overtaking the world, and perhaps even the consciousness of humanity. Remember, beloved of God, to have faith in your brothers and sisters on this plane. God has faith in all of them, in all of you. There will always be evil, for it is intrinsic to the balance of the Universe. Acknowledge it as a force, a presence, but know that you always retain the awesome power to choose love instead. And in every loving choice you make, you move closer to God, and take another step on your own path to enlightenment.

ON SPIRITUAL WORK IN THE MODERN WORLD

The work of the spirit is not difficult. Humans make it more difficult because they question everything in their lives. Why am I here? Why am I doing this? What purpose does this serve? What you always need to remember is that your purpose serves God, ultimately and intimately. You would not be on the Earth plane unless you made a choice—a choice to incarnate at this time, in this place, to learn lessons and work toward your own spiritual advancement. God understands this, for God gives you the impetus to pursue this noble goal. Spiritual enlightenment is the true goal of all people, even those who do not remember it after they return to the physical body. Some souls become so involved in and seduced by the creature comforts of the physical world that they cannot focus on their true nature—their spiritual essence and the soul lessons they incarnated in order to learn. They always have the free will to overcome these temptations and to achieve forward motion in their spiritual journey. Prayer helps this. If there is someone in your life who seems stuck in the mundane world, who becomes entangled in the negative energy and the obstacles that seem to constantly plague him, send prayers for this soul. Your prayers will help lift him out of the negative energy and set him back on a better path.

Pay attention to the children in your life. Notice how they adapt to the world around them and how they seem to absorb the energies surrounding them. They have not learned how to build defenses against any type of energy. So it is vital to surround children with positive energies, positive forces, and to encourage their own spiritual understanding. Children are not stupid creatures; they understand on their own intrinsic level who God is and how God is present within them. They connect very easily with this essential idea. The world into which they come, however, is not ideal, and their innocence, simplicity, and truly spiritual natures are often maimed or killed because adults do not understand how to nurture their souls. Do not bombard children with violent images or noisy surroundings. They do not need constant stimulation, as the modern world seems to advocate. Younger and younger children are thrust into noisy, bright, and overwhelming environments that actually harm their souls instead of helping them. Many humans seem to believe that they are advancing children's education by exposing them to these energies, but while their intellect may expand, their soul education, their spiritual advancement, erodes. Do not do this to the children who will be responsible for the direction of the planet in the future.

The children coming into the world at this time are exceptional. They are the Crystal and Indigo children so many talk about, and they will exhibit many attributes, mentally, emotionally, and spiritually, that will stun and awe many who meet them. They are the leaders of the next spiritual revolution, and they will not be like the children from the past. They are coming in on a special energy vibration because their expertise and compassion are needed in the world at this time. They do not require the same type of education as the children of the past, a fact that will be different and scary for those in power in school settings. The adult population needs to recognize and work toward better educational opportunities for all children, and this phenomenon will help them do that.

As for yourself—be as a child. Children know that they are loved by their parents; even in abusive households, they never question that their parents love them. Adults need to recognize that God, as Divine Parent, loves humanity with all its flaws and weaknesses. God also knows the unlimited capacity and potential of His creations, and He hopes, as all parents do, that His children will make wise choices that will bring them closer to achieving their goals. God never gives up on you; do not give up on God.

ON THE NATURE OF CREATOR

Feel the love you have for your own children—allow that feeling to fill you up, to consume you. Feel the joy that love brings to you, the intense happiness. This is how God feels every moment of every day about you, His children. Even when you do something disappointing, it is this intense love that God feels, the forgiveness of all wrongs, the drive to help you understand His love and this feeling, that He wishes to impart to one and all.

ON THE NATURE OF METATRON HIMSELF

I have always been here and will continue on into all eternity. Energy can change, but it never ends. All have been here since the beginning of time and will continue on, becoming. We are all becoming Divine. We are ever moving toward Divinity. There are so many worlds, dimensions that you may never see nor understand. Focus on the task at hand. I AM. You ARE. I AM here for all to know who wish to understand.

ON THE NUMBER ELEVEN AS A SIGNAL

Awakening comes through healing and the creation of balance. See the symbolism in the number eleven. This number signals changes in the pattern of life. From the point when it becomes apparent, there is no going backward. There is only forward motion. Consciousness expands and synchronicities abound as reminders of the soul's evolution. Beloved, do not expect others to journey with you. You are alone but for the spiritual helpers surrounding you, energies that support you in your quest. The number eleven is a reminder of patterns in human life that repeat, create, and re-create. What will you create? It is all up to you.

Q and A with Metatron

As I pursued this writing project, people began asking me what my next book was about. When I told them it focused on the Archangel Metatron and how seekers could get closer to his energy, many people seemed intrigued, posing additional and sometimes complicated questions. Some of the questions centered on Metatron himself, his nature and purpose. Others addressed his thoughts on world events, spiritual progression, and humanity's role and mission in the world, similar to my own musings featured earlier in this chapter. These broader questions left me feeling inadequate in some ways, because I had no idea how to answer them. I regretted having to tell the questioner, "I really don't know."

Finally, a solution came to me: let the Archangel answer the questions himself through the process of inspirational writing. Thank goodness Metatron was willing to reveal this solution, and I thank him for his willingness to work through me to bring the following answers to light.

The questions in the next pages were sent to me by people in my church community and by others I have taught in classes and lectures. Some of the questions were similar to those I had addressed earlier with Metatron, but many were quite different, reflecting varied points of view. (In a few cases, questions have been paired when they address similar subjects.) Metatron himself chose which questions to answer, and I served as the conduit through inspirational writing.

Many of these topics certainly provoke thought and
remind us of our personal responsibility in making our lives
and our world a better place.

Q.

I know that Metatron was the prophet Enoch. How or why
was he chosen to be an Archangel? Why does he have so
many names?

A.

I thank you for your excellent question, although I
prefer to focus not on my own nature and self, but
on you and your needs. I understand human curiosity, however, because angels are curious at times,
too. It is also within our nature to want to understand all of creation. As an Archangel of the highest sphere, I was created to serve God and to serve
humanity. This is my primary task, and it is one
I relish, for it keeps me always in the vibration of
God's incredible love. Because I wanted to be more
in tune with the needs and thoughts of humanity,
I discussed this with Creator, and I was given the
opportunity to incarnate into the physical realms as
the one called Enoch, whom you mention. I lived
many years on the Earth plane, and while I did so,
many others took up my angelic duties in these
heavenly spheres. While on Earth, I learned many
things about human behavior and belief, and these
are lessons I still carry with me. I use this experience

to help other angels understand and care better for their human charges.

Never doubt that these things are possible, because God is able to do so much more than the human mind can imagine! God wishes nothing as much as for you all to be comfortable, happy, and connected to Him, which is why He has commissioned the angelic kingdom to await your call and to attend to your needs. We do this because we love God and we love humanity, and we thank you for the opportunity to serve. My coming to Earth in the body called Enoch served that purpose, and this is why it was so. Not many angels have done so, because it is unnecessary for every angelic entity to have this experience, just as it is unnecessary for every human being to experience poverty in his lifetime. Angels are unique creations just as you are, and we are also learning our own lessons. This was one of mine, one I joyfully accepted as part of my experience of God and of myself.

Angels sometimes appear in humanity as people, but this is simply a façade we use so as not to overwhelm you with our appearance and high vibration energy. Some people would be stricken with fear and terror if they were to see angels in their true energy forms. You have read stories of angels appearing on the Earth plane to assist people? These are the stories where the angels appear out of nowhere and disappear when they are finished helping, yes? In these cases, my angelic brethren have assumed a physical body to perform the task at hand and to help the person in question understand that she is not alone. If we were to simply appear as energy, the person in need of help might simply faint or become so overwhelmed that it would be impossible to help her. Thus, we come "as angels unawares," that is, hidden within a human appearance. But we are there!

As you can see, I was neither chosen to be an Archangel, nor was I chosen to incarnate. I was created as an Archangel and Seraph, as you were created as a human being. Part of my natural progression as a spiritual being was to come to the Earth plane as a man for a time; this is not part of every angel's progression, nor may it be part of yours to become an angel, as seems to be a popular belief among humans. However, always remember that nothing is impossible with God, so do not rule out any possibility! Simply know what is "usual" and what is rare.

My name is Metatron. There are many variations on that name, as on yours: Cindy. Cindi. Cindie. They are simply variant spellings and have no other real relevance. I will, however, answer any call made to me. It is unnecessary to even know my name for me to understand the need someone has for me and the energy I can lend.

Q.

Have there been any recent angel incarnations into our world? Can angels still incarnate in this day and age, and do they? If so, are there any limitations or special rules they must follow?

A.

More excellent discussion on the incarnation of angels. It is so interesting to me that you all are so interested in us. Yes, there have been other angelic incarnations, although it is not within my nature to tell you when and how those have come about. There have been several human beings with "angelic" natures who have come into being because they asked, as their angelic selves, to experience human trials and challenges, and God granted them this. I stress again to you that this is not a "normal" process for an angel to undergo, so please do not think that all angels incarnate, nor do humans become angels in the heavenly planes as a rule of thumb, as you call it. There are no special rules or limitations here, because the Universe is limitless, and the only limitations placed upon it are those imposed by Natural Law. However, most angels are satisfied within their own selves to progress and work as they need to as angel energies.

Understand that for an angel to incarnate as a human is, for you, comparable to experiencing life on another planet as an alien species. Much thought must be given to this undertaking, and much intro-spection as to why it would serve humanity and the angelic realms for this to happen. I AM Meta-tron, close to God, but I AM not God Himself, so I have not the answers as to why this would serve all of creation. In every instance, I can assure you that the angels who have incarnated have done so to advance the state of humanity in some special and important way.

In your world at this time, there are no angelic incarnations, because the vibration of humanity is changing in such a way that they are not currently necessary. I AM aware that some believe them-selves or others to be angelic incarnations, but this is a misunderstanding of the heightened human energy vibration incarnating and/or accelerating at this time. Humanity is moving forward in its spiri-tual progression, which is what needs to happen. More people are aware of their connections to the angels, which is a step in the right direction, and more people can and do honor this connection, which thus links them back to God as well. Angelic incarnations are not necessary when humanity can recognize its own strengths and its own weak-nesses, which is part of the wisdom that is coming to humanity at this time. There is still a long way to go for the human race, but the progress is there. Have faith that you are advancing in exactly the right way and toward the correct purpose!

Q.

What role will angels and Archangels have in the future? Will it be different from what it has been in the past?

Q.

Why haven't more angels incarnated? With all the turmoil in the world, sometimes it's hard to see the angels' presence. How can we see signs that they are truly around us and helping to ease all the suffering in the world? How do angels interact with us from day to day? Do they work with us through our spirit guides, or do they work with us directly?

A.

I AM pleased to answer your questions about angels and our purpose in the Universe. Sometimes those of us in the angelic kingdom become disheartened because more human beings do not recognize our presence. This is not an attachment to ego, because angels do not have ego in the same sense that humans do. We are sometimes concerned that people are unaware of us because we are your helpers, and we want to aid each of you in the achievement of your spiritual goals. This is one of the primary purposes of angels, and we humbly and happily perform these duties with and for you as you give us the permission to do so.

Herein lies the most important piece: you must ask for our presence, and you must allow us to help you. We are not able to work without your permission. Sometimes we intercede when an unconscious permission is given, and this is sometimes seen by observers as a miracle healing or occurrence. What needs to be recognized is that in these instances, the people who are saved or helped have actually asked for this intercession at a soul level, even if they cannot recognize at a mental level that they have asked for aid. This is why you may not have an awareness of our presence, especially when times seem so difficult and tumultuous. The signs are there, but they are often small and perhaps difficult to ascertain.

This is not because we are trying to make things hard for you. It is because the impulse you sent out, the frequency of your asking, was not made with the most sincere faith and trust. So many of you half-heartedly believe in us, instead of having true faith in our abilities to help you. This incomplete trust is sent out as your thought or prayer energy, and in accordance with the Natural Law of Vibration, this is the energy that returns to you. The answer that you seek, or the help that you need, can only be returned to you on the same energy vibration. We want to send a stronger signal, so you must try to reach for your highest and best belief and joy and send that assurance out. This way, the answer will be more noticeable and more easily understood. The more you ask, the more we will answer, and the more you will understand and appreciate our presence in the world.

Angels can and do interact with humanity on an everyday basis. Carry us with you in your heart every moment of every day, and realize the potential for aid that we have. We will always answer every call that comes to us, but keep in mind the Law of Vibration that we already discussed. Keep your mind centered on what you need to achieve and see it as if it has already come into your material world. This way, the answer can manifest in a more tangible way, and our answers to you can become less subtle and more pronounced. Trust that we are with you. Believe in the unseen, because we are here, even when we are not noticeable. We angels know that this is difficult for you all, who have been raised on science and taught to believe only your eyes. You must teach your children to believe their hearts, for this is how the Messengers of God speak to each of you. Hear me, for I speak true.

All angels are elated to work directly with human beings. Your spirit guides are wonderful helpers, too, and can understand human needs sometimes better than angelic workers. However, angels have been given by God an express purpose to fulfill—to serve humanity and the Universe that God created. This is our ultimate purpose, and we rejoice when human beings allow us to work in this purpose. Enlist our guidance and help so that we can all work together to make the Universe a better, more enlightened, and loving energy.

Our roles as angels are revealed to us as God's purpose unfolds. Like you, sometimes we come to points in our existence that take us in different directions. This is why and when some angels may incarnate on the physical plane, as I once did for my own spiritual progression. This is not a common occurrence, as I mentioned in a previous communication. No one, not even the highest Archangel, knows completely the Mind of God, and I do not pretend to understand every aspect of God's purpose for either humanity, the angelic kingdom, or any of God's beloved creations. I can tell you that angels continue to work at enhancing the love vibration of the Universe as we always have, in all of our interactions with humanity, no matter what their level. Angels channel love to all aspects of the Earth plane; we change vibrations when we can to match the love vibration of the higher realms so that all creation can experience God's love as much as it chooses to, as often as possible. We seek to bring all of the planes into harmony in that love vibration. This is one of our most important tasks, and this is how we are able to work individually with every human being. When human energy vibrations harmonize with God's loving vibration, the Universe aligns, and all creation moves forward in its unique spiritual progression.

Do you see how important maintaining that love energy truly is? The function of the Universe relies on it. All advancement relies on it. We angels work with you all for the advancement of the greater good and the overarching energy of All That Is.

Q.

How can I learn to trust my communication with my own spiritual guides? What does the communication look, sound, feel like?

A.

It is good that you ask today about how you personally can recognize communications from the higher realms, for this is essential to your own growth and progression as a spiritual being. So many human beings believe in the sacred writings that have been passed down through many generations, but they do not believe that the communication process through which these texts came continues today. Beloved beings, why would communication stop? Why would God, who so loves you and wants more than anything for you to experience your connection to Him, end these communications at the time of Christ, or Muhammad, or Buddha, or any of the great human Masters who walked on the Earth? If this does not make sense to you, it is because it is not truth. Truth resonates in your heart. The truth is that God does communicate to each of you. He uses many means to do this, including but not limited to your guides and teachers and those of us in the angelic kingdom. We are Messengers to your own truth.

Your question is a common one, and it exemplifies how difficult it is for human beings to trust. Many human beings do not recognize their connection to Divinity. They see themselves as human and God as Divine, and they believe, because they were taught this from a young age, that God is separate from themselves. This is a flawed teaching. God is NEVER separate from you. Each of you is connected to God and thus Divine in your own right. You can never dislodge the sacred Divinity within yourself, not even if you perform the most heinous acts or crimes while on the Earth plane. Why does this connection not disappear? Because God wants every person to always have the opportunity to reconnect with Him. I have spoken to you about choice. You always have a choice to return to God. You always have a choice to love and to live in that loving vibration that is God by making good, loving choices in your life. In the same way that you can never be disconnected from your own Divinity, you can never be disconnected from your ability to communicate with the Messengers who wish to help you during your struggles and issues while you remain in the physical body. God has commissioned the angels, your guides and teachers, and the Masters to help humanity. The way that they can help is by sending you guidance and signals when you need assistance. This constant wave of energy is always present. Now, you must learn how to "tune in" to this energy, much as you tune in to a radio station, as you say.

I have spoken before about keeping your energy vibration high by remaining in a loving state. When you are in a loving state, you cannot help but exude a more loving aura and energy to everything around you. It follows, then, that when you ask for guidance for yourself and you ask in this loving vibration, the answer will come to you more strongly and you will recognize the answer more easily. You must EXPECT the answer to come, and you must allow for it to come to you in many ways. Never try to limit the way the angels or your spirit teachers can bring information to you. Perhaps the easiest way for them to get a message to you is through a song on your radio as you drive in your car. They move the vibrations around you so that the next song that plays is pertinent to your situation and the question you asked. You hear the song on the radio as you drive and you think, "Well, isn't that funny? I asked if I should go into business with John, and the song playing on the radio is 'Johnny B. Goode.' What a coincidence." No, beloved! It is NOT a coincidence! We angels constantly hear our beloved human beings saying, "There are no coincidences," and yet, when something like this happens, the first thought that goes through that same human's head is "What a coincidence." I chuckle with you as you read this, because

I know it is hard. Remember: if you ask for guidance, you must EXPECT to receive it, and do not allow your own mind to LIMIT how the guidance will come. Many times, guidance will present itself in a humble way, so you must pay attention. This engages all of your senses. You might think this makes it harder, and we do not wish to make things more challenging to you. However, you have not followed through on your end of the equation. Look, listen, feel . . . these senses are all imperative. Use them. Once you have asked for guidance, EXPECT that it will come, and open all of your senses to receive the message. And you can always ask that the answer will be sent in a way that you will understand.

Work with your spirit guides and angels on trust and faith. So many humans have issues with this. Many times, this stems from trust issues that you have with other human beings. You must remember that God is NOT another human being. If you have problems trusting because you were once involved in a love relationship with an unfaithful partner, this may color all of your human relationships. But remember, beloved, that God is NOT human. God is always faithful and always loving. He will not betray you. And neither will the Messengers who have been commissioned to help you. Concentrate on raising your vibration and aligning it in a loving way with God's ultimate loving energy, and the answers to your questions will be clearer.

Q.

Sometimes, when I look back on my day, I may realize that because I wasn't feeling good, or had a bad day, I had a lot of negative thoughts. I pray to the angels and guardians to transform those negative thoughts into positive energies. Can the angels really help us in that way?

A.

Beloved, thank you for this question, which is of vital importance to all who wish to grow spiritually. It is normal for humans to have an occasional bad day, and in the course of this, to harbor negative thoughts and feelings. The most important thing to remember is that within every moment of every day, you have the awesome power to change your thoughts, to change your emotion and your mood, to rise out of these negative vibrations, and to dwell in a harmonious, loving, positive energy vibration! This power is yours alone; the angels, myself included, can help facilitate this process by helping change the energy that surrounds you.

But please remember that the angels can only work within Natural Law. We can change the energy around you, but if you continue to wallow in negative vibrations, you will never feel the positive energy we have tried to bring to you, because you will be attracting through your own thoughts and energies the very same negative vibrations you already feel. All angels want you to call on us, for we are happy to help in any way we can. However, we cannot change

your thoughts, and thus cannot always make a significant difference in the vibrations you attract, because
changing your thoughts and in turn your emotions
is within your own power. It is not within ours. We
can help you RELEASE negative thoughts, and as
you let go of them, we can help change those negative energies that you release in meditation, prayer,
and ritual into positive energies. So do continue to
call on us, and ask us to help you RELEASE all negative thought patterns so that your mood and emotion will be elevated to a more positive place. This
way, you will then attract more positive energies into
your field, and you will feel better and more peaceful
throughout your day.

Q.

Are we all moving toward dwelling in a state of perfect
love, a state where even all our thoughts are pure? Can it
mean gaining back lost innocence?

A.

This is a most interesting question. Thank you for
posing it, as the nature of humanity's Divinity is of
utmost importance as you continue to grow and
progress.

Within the realm of Divine Consciousness, there
is naught but love. Within this state, All That Is
functions from a consciousness of purity and bliss.
This is what the love vibration is truly all about. It is

simple, and yet it is a very difficult state to achieve, because all thoughts, all intelligence, all Mind, must be released and surrendered to truly meld into this perfect state of Being.

Innocence implies a state of non-intelligence, the state of one who has not yet learned. Most human beings think of a child when they think of innocence. A child has not yet learned all he or she must in order to function in a human state. Once the child learns certain things, he or she is no longer innocent. He or she cannot go backward and unlearn those things that have been taught. The same is true of spiritual progression. A soul can never go backward; it can only journey forward toward ultimate Divinity, or it can move laterally and stay in the same energy vibration it currently dwells in, not moving forward in a spiritual progression. So, in a literal sense, gaining All That Is does not include returning to innocence, which would, in essence, mean beginning over again.

In dwelling in the state of All That Is, there is no thought separate from God. The soul becomes one with Creator and experiences the essence of connection with that Source that sustains All That Is. It is often a difficult state to describe, because human beings cannot relate to it, other than through fleeting feelings of transcendence that they may have experienced on the Earth plane. I can tell you that in that Source energy, All is love, infinitely and without end. Nothing can dwell in love that is not of love. This is the state that all are trying to return to, the place where God has no measure, no boundaries, no beginning and no end.

Q.

I am sometimes confused by the experience of pleasurable sensations. For example, kissing and hugging are pleasurable experiences. Drinking and smoking are pleasurable to some people but can be physically destructive. How can we keep from harming ourselves? I would like to better understand how the physical body interacts with our mind/ego, which can be destructive. Is ego necessary? How can we understand and embrace our ego? How can we dissolve the imperfections of our mind yet be loving and grateful for its use as a tool?

A.

Thank you for bringing up this interesting topic for discussion. I AM happy to work with you in finding answers to these questions.

You touch on something that troubles many who journey on a spiritual path. What is the purpose of the physical, of the body? How can you separate the physically pleasurable from the spiritual, for they must be separate, yes?

Let me begin by saying: beloved child, you are in the body because you chose to be in the body. You came into this physical incarnation because you wanted, for whatever reason, to have a physical experience. A physical experience thus renders all physical sensations such as the ones you describe as an essential part of your humanity. Are some physical experiences "better" or "more spiritual" than others? Creator would not judge them as so, and so you should not judge them this way, either. Physical acts are sometimes pleasurable and sometimes painful. It is their nature, and the key to understanding them is to understand your desire for them and what their purpose is.

Remember, beloved: Creator wants you to be happy, and part of being happy in the physical body is experiencing pleasure through that instrument. So you have intimacy with others, you have foods that you eat that you enjoy, you have sports and entertainment where you use your body in a fashion that elevates your mood. Is there something wrong with this? No. The challenge sometimes comes when something that is perceived as being "wrong" or "sinful" begins to become an obsession, an addiction, or a physical need that you cannot deny.

Take alcohol, for instance. Is it a bad thing to have a glass of wine or a mixed drink? For many people, no. Alcohol relaxes the body, making it feel better after a stressful time. Is it bad for someone to enjoy alcohol on a regular basis? For many people, no. Is it bad for someone to become addicted to alcohol? Creator would not call it "bad" or "sinful." Creator looks with love on all of His children, and an addiction, the result of poor choices, would not make Creator love this addicted child any less. The addict, however, must then overcome many challenges and obstacles in order to bring himself back into a state of balance and peace. This is, of course, very possible.

So is the physical experience of drinking alcohol a bad thing? No, it is not. Even over-drinking is not a bad thing, because there is no judgment concerning these actions. What is important is how the human being became entrenched in this cycle of abuse, and what steps can be taken to bring him back into balance. This is one of the great challenges of the human existence, for every person must remember that he is a spiritual being within a physical body. When you can make choices in your life based on love (not love of a physical sensation, but loving yourself as well as others), then you are making progress as a spiritual being. The body is not your enemy, nor are pleasures that may come from using your body. It is important, however, to always think through choices and to see where the end result may leave you, physically and spiritually.

You ask about ego. Yes, ego is a necessary component to the human experience. If you had no ego, you would not have free will or free choice, which is so important to the spiritual progression of the soul. It is easy to make a choice if there are no repercussions, and thus there is no growth. Ego helps human beings define themselves as separate individuals. If there was no ego, there would be no separation of souls, and this is also vital, as every soul must progress at its own rate and within its nuanced purpose. Many equate ego with feelings of supremacy or power, but this is not the case for most people. Ego helps you make choices, so eliminating it would not serve you as free will beings.

Many of the great human Masters understood that each human soul is individual and thus should shine in its own unique way. Recognizing this is how you can embrace and love your ego. Your ego helps you define who you are at your deepest essence. It helps you find your purpose in your life mission on Earth. When this is done from a loving vibration rather than a selfish one, then your ego is truly helping you progress on your spiritual journey.

Yes, the mind may be perceived as imperfect. If it were completely realized, beloved, you would not be in the physical body, but instead be melded with All That Is, the Mind of God! Since you are in the body, recognizing the great gift that your intellect provides is vital to your understanding of your progression. The intellect is only a PART of the mind. Your scientists say that a human being only uses five percent of her mind. What is going on in all the other parts? One of the great challenges, and one of the exciting frontiers in science, is the exploration of the human mind. There are worlds in there, as there are worlds within the Universe, and by accessing those energies and those places in the mind, these other planes can also be seen and experienced. The mind of humanity is modeled after the Mind of God. What has sprung forth from the Mind of God? Nothing short of a Universe filled with infinite possibilities! So it is with the mind of humanity. So much can be achieved. You are all working toward this, and the knowledge is beginning to be accessed more frequently and taught to others so that they may benefit as well.

You have incarnated at a very exciting time, beloved one! Continue to study the mind, and you will have better access to its potential. Do not view it as an imperfect tool, for what you think, you become. Say, "My mind is perfect, and I understand all of the infinite possibilities that it holds." Thus, you create a loving vibration for this knowledge to come to you . . . and come it will.

Q.

I have been told that more and more people are "waking up." Why is this happening now?

A.

Those with whom you have been conversing on this subject speak the truth. Humanity is coming into an age now where more spiritual pursuits will be given the importance and the energy that is necessary for progression to take place. It is an exciting time to be in the physical body, beloved child of God! Your scientists continue to make great advances in the field of human energy and the mind, and these discoveries encourage others to seek and find answers to age-old questions.

This is also happening now because more and more people have made a conscious choice to share the information they are receiving. For a long period of time, great spiritual discoveries were not shared with others because those who possessed the knowledge were afraid of the consequences this would bring to them. They had reason to fear, because so many in power were determined to increase their own status and to keep others in a lowly position. This was a sad time, indeed, and there are still elements of this energy present on the Earth plane today.

Many souls, however, are awakening to the concept that their Divinity has never been separate from them. God is within. God cannot be found without, at least not in the way some people seek Him. Comfort and community is one thing when seeking God, but ultimately, a soul must find God within itself. This is what is now happening, because more people are making conscious choices to live in love. When they consciously choose love over fear, they move closer energetically to their own Divinity, and thus begin to understand, or "wake up," to the concept that they ARE DIVINE. There was not a timeline in existence as to when this would happen to humanity. It, as everything, is set into motion by God, and progression occurs as human beings are ready to make loving choices. Those of us in the angelic kingdom congratulate and honor all of you for the steps you are taking toward this great awakening!

Q.

How can we reconcile the belief in a spiritual plane of existence, which is inhabited by the spirits of deceased people, spirit guides, angels and (presumably) demons, with the desire to obtain objective empirical evidence of such a realm? Will our measurement devices ever be calibrated to the degree that is necessary to capture (and display!) the information that will provide incontrovertible evidence?

A.

Beloved child, never think for an instant that God desires to keep you all in the dark about the many wonders of His Universe! He is working with your great scientists every day to aid them in their studies, their discoveries, and their quest to understand the intricacies of the many planes of existence. Your field of quantum physics is the new frontier of this type of work, and many advances will continue to be made well into the future. I, a humble angel, cannot foresee what future humankind will have in relation to these discoveries, simply because that all hinges on free will and the decisions of these scientific minds to pursue these admirable goals. I can tell you, however, that there are many now who see the usefulness of such studies and are on the brink of making important breakthroughs in their research. It follows that it is only a matter of time before these planes are seen and measured in some way.

As for reconciling your belief in the unseen worlds with your need for scientific data to support it: God desires faith, but not at the cost of undermining your own needs as human souls to learn and grow and study. God created humanity with intellect and free will, and it is up to each individual soul to use or not to use either gift. Sometimes faith demands that you believe in that which cannot be proven. It does not dictate, however, that it will NEVER be proven. And so I commend you for your question, and I say to you in truth: there is no timeline. There is no set agenda for what will be accomplished and what will not. There is only the individual soul and its progression, and its learning that it is Divine.

Q.

What is a miracle? Why do we not see the old-fashioned Bible kind of miracles in the world today? Or is it just that we aren't observant?

A.

Your insight is apparent, beloved one, when you notice that human beings are not very observant at times while in the body. What you call miracles happen every moment of every day on the Earth plane, and yet they go virtually unnoticed. There are healings of individual people who were thought to be on the brink of transition. There are rescues of children from terrible situations of poverty or abuse. There are souls in the body that are able to perform great feats that you call bi-location, materialization, and the like, events that would stun your scientists and baffle many of your great thinkers. Why do these go unnoticed, especially in an age in your world where information is so accessible and easily traded?

It all goes back to the choices that some are making. Your news media chooses not to report on these types of stories, ones that would make the human spirit soar. Instead it highlights violence, death, and despair. This makes the angels sad, but we recognize that this is a great challenge to humanity. These choices mostly come from greed, not from true malice. People who have experienced miracles often choose fear and so do not share their miraculous events because they are afraid others will ridicule them or call them fraudulent or dishonest. The angels bless those who have come forward to tell their stories, because these travel and touch their listeners, and this raises the vibration of the whole Universe to one that is closer to love rather than to fear. There will always be those who doubt the existence of God, the intercession of angels, and the miraculous power of healing that Creator can bring and manifest in each and every person. So it always has been, even at the time of the Bible of which you speak. Do you not think the Master Jesus had those who doubted, ridiculed, hated the healings and other miracles performed through him? This is one reason he frightened those in power, and they chose to put him to death. Another choice based on fear. Think what Jesus may have been able to teach these other souls had they chosen love instead and opened their hearts and minds to the power he wanted to share with them!

Remember that "miracle" is a human term, used to define something that seems to defy explanation. There is always an explanation that moves in accordance with Natural Law, the tenets that Creator has set up to keep the Universe in order and motion. Humanity may never completely understand all of these Laws and how they may produce such "miraculous" ends, and yet your scientists are beginning to see the key components of how these Laws operate. Progress is being made; rejoice in that, as we angels do!

Q.

What are the best ways to prove our spirit guides and angels exist to people who don't see them or refuse to believe they exist? Why is it so hard to believe that they exist? Why can't everyone see or feel them? Why can't they just prove themselves by appearing?

A.

So many questions, beloved ones! Let me see if I can assuage some of your curiosity.

When you speak of Spirit, I AM convinced you mean those souls that have passed into the etheric realms after the death of their physical bodies. These souls have become pure energy once again, and energy is always accessible. Your scientists mention this. It is within the grasp of every human being to be able to communicate with these energies even though they are in another realm. This is because all is based on the Natural Law of Vibration. Those in the world of spirit can communicate, but not all realize this, nor do all choose to do so. The same is true of human beings still in the physical body. Once again, the exercising of free will is the issue. Can every person see and feel these souls? Yes, they can, although they may choose not to, or they may choose not to learn about this process to make it accessible to them. Bravo to them for exercising their free will! Would God choose to open their eyes so that they can see the beauty and the advancement that would come to humanity if these realms were acknowledged and accessed more often? God has never done this before, because this would interfere with the free will of His creations. It is up to the individual soul to learn and grow.

Human beings naturally tend to only believe in what they can experience tangibly, through the senses of sight, hearing, taste, touch, and smell. Most rely primarily on sight, hearing, and touch. They also rely most heavily on science, which tells them that if they cannot see, hear, or touch it, it does not exist. So they have been ingrained with logic, and spiritual progression is not always logical! And so, many human beings have an encounter with a loved one who has passed, or with an angel, and they rationalize it, saying, "That could not have been my dead father in the room with me, even though it certainly looked like him. It was dark, though—I probably made it up because I miss him." This is not the fault of the soul who worked so hard to make itself known! Nor is it really the fault even of the one who chooses not to believe. It is simply where his soul is in its progression at this time, and all is Divinely Right at all times.

It is challenging for those souls who have returned to pure energy to manifest in your physical realm. This requires a great deal of power and manipulation of that energy field, and some souls do not believe they can generate the power necessary to do this. Do you see how they are also still evolving? They are like many of you, who do not realize the potential that they have within them as Divine Beings. Once that power is discovered, however, on the path of spiritual progression, the soul unites once more with Creator, never to be separated. And so, the soul would not then appear anyway. Some souls are able to manifest and choose to do so, and angels manifest quite frequently, as do the Ascended Masters and Master energies that work with humanity. We often go unrecognized, however, for many human beings refuse to see what is right before them. Why? Mostly they refuse to see out of fear, which we have discussed at length in previous communications.

And so I say truly to you, beloved ones: concern yourselves not with what others believe to be true. Live your truth as best you can, in love, and you will continue to progress as you should.

Q.

Is the activation of the Golden Christ Grid for the advancement of humanity into the higher dimensions proceeding as it was planned?

A.

Thank you for your question, beloved one. It is obvious that you are a lightworker and well versed in many areas of spiritual thought and discussion about the progression of humanity. The one with whom I work is not familiar with this concept, and so I do the best I can to convey to you through her what I know to be true concerning your inquiry.

The Golden Christ Grid of which you speak is an energy that has been worked on for a long period of time, whether measured in human terms or in the spirit realms. It has been known by other names, but no name is more important than the energy that is building because of the concentration and effort given to it. The Enlightened Ones known by some as the Great White Brotherhood are the keepers of these sacred energies and efforts, and these beings work closely with all, whether they are aware of their help or not, who truly seek the perfection of the human state, the Earth planes, and the Divine connection of humanity with All That Is. This is not an area that the angels oversee, although there are angels who work with some of the other energies to continue to build and raise the energy necessary to affect the human consciousness. I AM aware of much extra energy currently channeling to this effort because so many more human beings are tuning their own vibrations into higher thought patterns based on love, compassion, understanding, charity, and other noble aims.

Humanity is progressing in its awareness of spiritual matters, which thus moves the entire advancement of humanity further along the path to enlightenment. The Grid, as you call it, helps to further focus this energy, and as the love vibration strengthens, the Grid becomes more powerful and brings about more advancement. Some people enjoy visualizing this process, for it helps them focus their thoughts and energies in a positive way. You are welcome to do this if you like. Know that all is progressing at its best pace, for all is in alignment with Creator and His Divine purpose.

Q.

Please comment on the metaphysical theory that we plan
our lives before we even get here.

A.

I AM happy, beloved child, to comment on this matter that is on your mind. The process of incarnation
for the human soul is a beautiful one infused with
the loving, compassionate, supportive energy of
Creator God, who rejoices any time a soul decides
to put on a physical body for an experience on the
Earth plane. Yes, each soul energy may decide, if
she chooses, to incarnate into a physical experience. Since the soul is given this free-will option,
it stands to reason that the soul is also given freedom to choose certain experiences she wishes to
have while in the body. Often, the soul meets with
advisors, spirit guides, and Master teachers in order
to decide which lessons need to be addressed
given the progression of that individual soul and
what has already been learned or not learned in
previous incarnations. This is an exciting process
for every soul that chooses it, for the opportunity
to progress is what draws every soul to this decision, and the yearning to move closer to Creator
and His Divine energy is a loving motivation. And
so the soul chooses a specific circle of souls within
which to incarnate; she chooses her soul path to the
extent that the lessons she needs to learn will be

presented to her in myriad ways throughout her life. Understand, however, that at any time during her lifetime, the soul may choose another path, another direction, another person in the physical body and turn her back on all the ones she chose while in the spirit planes, because she can always exercise free will, no matter what.

Say, for example, this beloved soul chooses to incarnate in a poverty-stricken country, born to uneducated, miserable parents. Perhaps she chose this path because she wanted to learn about lack so that she could use the incredible power of her own Divinity to overcome it. Perhaps this is chosen as her life path purpose or mission, and so she is born with an incredible desire to move beyond the place of her bodily birth and to a place where she can receive an education. At fifteen years of age, she is faced with a choice: marry a boy from her village and spend the rest of her life scraping out her existence, or leave her village to attend a school three hundred miles away. Which will she choose? It is up to her! Her life plan before incarnating may have been to overcome lack, but she could very well choose to marry and stay where she is. If she chooses this, will she have other opportunities in her lifetime to carry out her life plan? Yes. The Universe will bring similar opportunities to her, for this is what she asked for at her most basic, soul level, and the Universe will respond in kind. Will she make a different choice the next time? Perhaps. Perhaps not. It is up to her! God, the angels, her beloved spirit teachers—none of these energies can force her to choose differently, even if it means helping her to advance more quickly. She must always choose, and choose she shall, whether she understands that it is a choice or not. And so her soul progresses, either in baby steps or in great leaps, based on her choices while in the body.

I hear what some of you may ask next: "Metatron, do we choose when and how we will die?" Ah, beloved children—there is so much fear of death, and yet, through death, you return to that which you are at your most intrinsic level: spirit. And yet, I understand why you may fear this transition. In your human experience, there are many kinds of deaths that seem violent, painful, or excruciatingly trying. Remember that God does not wish for any human soul to suffer and always gives tools to keep pain of any kind at bay. You may say, "But Metatron, my loved one suffered from cancer and died from it." Or, "My loved one passed in a terrible accident." Or even, "My loved one was murdered." Yes, terrible tragedies like murder and accidents and painful passings do occur. And yet it is important to look at all of these circumstances through Divine eyes, not human eyes. Perhaps a lingering passage was chosen by a soul so that others around him could learn from it. Maybe it gave all of the family members time to connect with each other and to appreciate the circle of loved ones. Perhaps a murder or an accident victim agreed before coming into the body that he would play that role for the one responsible for the death and teach her one of her important life lessons. Does this make the death any easier to accept? Perhaps not, but there is a reason, and one way to assuage grief is to find the Divine in all that comes to pass.

No matter what transition is agreed upon while the soul remains in the spirit planes, there may be adjustments made to the when and the how of the transition depending on what the soul learns while on the Earth plane. If a soul learns to trust God and believes in "miraculous" healing, a lesson in faith that she planned to experience, perhaps the cancer that engulfs her body at an early age will completely vanish, and she will have the opportunity to continue living in the body for many years to come. Perhaps then she will attract to herself a peaceful transition at a very advanced age, and this will be because she exercised her free will and transformed her belief system. What progression, then, that this soul has made! So it is possible to change any life, simply by exercising free will and understanding the Divine process of co-creation.

Q.

What happens to our souls as we evolve?

A.

What an extraordinary question you ask today! How to explain the process of soul progression? I will try my best to give you an answer, and it will be one that you will sit and contemplate for a time. Do not try too hard to understand, but see what feels right to you in these words and allow them to speak their truth to you in your body, in your soul.

I have spoken in previous communications about the process of a soul choosing to incarnate into a physical body. When it is time for the soul to come back to the spirit planes, his body dies, and his pure spirit returns to the etheric realms. Depending on the energetic vibration of his soul at the time of his transition, he is attracted to a certain plane of existence in the higher realms. Some may ask, "How many realms are there? How many planes?" Beloved, there are numerous experiences in the higher planes that a soul may attract through his energy vibration, and the correct, highest, and best plane for each individual soul will be the one to which he goes. There are many, many experiences the soul may have in a particular spirit realm, for they are all different in some ways. I shall not explain all the differences here, but know that these experiences of pure love energy are always perfect and complete for the souls that arrive there.

Once the soul has made this transition, and once his life-review and healing process takes place, he is then free to learn more and continue to grow spiritually. He may choose to rest for a period of time; he may choose to pray and commune with God as closely as possible; he may choose to attend the higher schools of learning available on the different planes of the spirit world; he may visit with other souls he recognizes. The list of activities that he may choose is endless. However, never doubt that the soul's progression continues in the spirit world. Every soul is moving ever closer to the Divine Power that is at the center of the Universe.

The soul, after time, may decide to assume another physical body and incarnate on the Earth plane again. The soul may decide to explore some of the other worlds in the spirit planes that are open to him at his progression level. And yet, no matter what he chooses, this soul is exactly where he needs to be in his own journey toward enlightenment.

Through many cycles of work, rest, study, play, travel, and the like, the soul may move into a state of complete union and understanding of his own Higher Power, his own Divinity. At this point, the soul has reunited completely with Creator, and he no longer separates himself in any way from the Divine. There will be no more incarnations for this soul, for he is at one with All That Is.

Q.

Are we still being visited by extraterrestrial beings as much in the past twenty years as we were previously?

Q.

Are there other life forms in other places—such as in other galaxies? Do the Creator and the angels help them also?

A.

I have asked the one with whom I work to put these two questions together so that I may address them as one concept. Yes, there are many, many worlds that connect within the grand space that is the Universe. The Universe is one with the Mind of God, and all of God's creations within it are interconnected. This is why some human souls can communicate easily with the angelic realms, some can communicate with those who are now pure energy after their death-transition, some can communicate with what human beings call aliens or extraterrestrials, some can communicate with elemental energies . . . the list goes on. All human souls, however, have the capacity to communicate and access all planes of existence. Will you do so in this lifetime? Perhaps not. It may well be that this is not in your life-plan, or within your realm of interest. It is important to remember that you are an evolving soul, and while all knowledge and all wisdom is open to you, it will most likely not come to you in one human lifetime.

I shall say, however, as I have said before: nothing is impossible with God, so do not rule this idea out! But the Messengers from the angelic kingdoms, as well as your spirit teachers and the great Masters of the human planes, are more readily accessible to you than you may know. Freely call upon their energies when you feel you need them, and trust that they will respond. This is how the Universe works at all levels: set your intention in the most loving vibration you can, and expect that what you ask for will come to you!

You ask about visitors to your planet. They are still among you, although you may not feel their energies as you once did. Recall that some are more in tune with these energies than others, and so some human beings may not feel them or believe in them at all. This does not mean that they do not exist, nor does it mean that they have stopped visiting. You have been blessed with a good experience in your visitations, and you understand these energies to be beneficial. Some humans, however, did not understand the visitations and interpreted them as a threat. They were and remain fearful of this contact, and so some of the "alien" souls do not come to you as frequently as they once did. If you open yourself to the possibility and intention of receiving these loving visitations again, then they will occur for you. You must send out the invitation now as a form of energy, much as you would telephone a friend to invite her to dine with you. Remember, too, that these "alien" energies are evolving on their spiritual paths as well, and so their interactions with human beings, while still possible, might not be the place where their focused energy should be at this time.

There are some in the angelic kingdom who work with energies in other worlds rather than the Earth plane. We are available to them as well, but they do not tend to focus on our energy very much. We are primarily focused on the human soul energy, since this is our intended purpose as God's Messengers. There are other beings that serve God and this population much better and with more energy than the angelic kingdom. Know this: Creator has a wide and varied Universe, and He loves all of His creations and works with all of them in the ways best suited for them.

Q.

What do you think is most important for a parent to understand and nurture in her children?

Q.

Please discuss the new children (Indigos, Rainbows, and Crystals) who are entering the planet and their purpose.

A.

I AM happy to discuss with you today, beloved children of Creator, the subject of your children, the little ones who come after you to inherit the Earth plane and to bring about their own spiritual progression. You mention the New Souls, the ones your writers and embodied spiritual teachers have called the Indigo, Crystal, and Rainbow children. It is indeed true that many of the souls incarnating on the Earth plane at this time, and throughout the last two decades (in your time measurement) are very special energies. These souls have chosen to incarnate at this time for many reasons, but partly because they belong to special soul groups that have taken it as part of their purpose and mission to help advance more rapidly the spiritual progression of the human race. This is not a mission that they take lightly; many of the souls now incarnating are very serious about their spiritual progression and about their purposes, even if they cannot accurately articulate these ideas when they first enter the body.

These children, however, are very advanced intellectually, for they remember better than some others the spirit planes and their own role in spiritual progression. Many of these children will show signs at young ages of intelligence and incredible creativity. They will also have many insights that will stun adults, and some elders will not understand or know how to interact with these energies. Many of these children may also exhibit what some adults would call behavior problems or challenges, but this is simply because their minds work so quickly and they easily become bored with routine tasks and uninspired endeavors. The greatest challenge for parents and teachers of these souls is that the current educational systems employed in many of your countries do not cater to the individual needs of these types of students, and thus many will be medicated or fail at studies, which decreases the benefit these souls may bring to humanity. This is one reason what you call home schooling has become so popular; many parents of these New Souls recognize that there is something different about their children, and they take them out of the traditional school setting in order to better engage these energies so that they can flourish.

With these children, great strides will be made in the areas of medicine, science, and especially spirituality. What will be most interesting is the emphasis that will be placed on the connection between the health of the soul and the health of the body, as well as the spiritual force that is behind all scientific matter and theory. These souls will also make greater strides in negotiations and peace efforts between nations of the world, but only if the adults who influence them at their younger ages emphasize respect and love for all beliefs and cultures. This is where parents and any adults who have contact with youngsters must focus their energy.

Teach your children love and respect. Show them by example that love and respect bring better and happier results for all. Teach them nonviolent ways of solving problems and conflicts. Encourage their creativity through music, art, and an appreciation for beauty. Love to be with them, and tell them this. Honor the Divine within them by teaching them about this concept: that God is within, so loving oneself is as important as loving one's neighbor. Help them to understand compassionate stewardship by taking care of the animals and environment that surrounds them. All of these are vital lessons that they will carry in their hearts as they grow older, and they, in turn, will pass these lessons on to the next generation.

Q.

How do we as humans get past the fear of the unknown in order to move on spiritually?

Q.

Many people have fears, both big and small, that keep us from achieving our potentials. I know that prayer and meditation are good ways to deal with these fears, but do you have any advice on how else to deal with our fears?

A.

Beloved of God, I AM happy to address your questions about fear. Fear is something I realize all humanity must face, but face it you must! It cannot be conquered if it is ignored or avoided. Face your fears head on, and know that the All supports you in your quest for truth and for courage. God is the ultimate source of strength, and when your faith is unwavering, your fear will be nonexistent. Remember that God realizes that faith is shaken by fear because there are many circumstances in your world that seem overwhelming. Yet you are always safe and protected by God, and the angels, no matter in which sphere they dwell, are at your service to provide the safety and the help that you need and seek. Call on us—it is not necessary to know our names. It is only necessary to know that we are real and do exist to serve you in love. This is our task—allow us to help and guide you. Give us your fears. Speak to

us in times of crisis, and we will help erase the anxi-
eties that you feel. But do not wait just for times of
crisis to realize that we are constant and true to you.
Ask for us to stay with you, to protect you and your
families, and you will start to see the difference that
asking for our help can bring. We cannot intervene
if you do not wish for it, so you must ask!

You mention prayer and meditation, so you
already know the very best ways to connect with the
Divine, with us, and with your own Higher Self. This
is also the best way to ask for help and for fear to be
removed. All you need to do is ask, and we will be
able to change the energies around you so that you
are not overcome by fear but instead feel a sense of
calm and peace. That is all that is needed—asking,
and expecting that this will be done for you. Accept
the energy that we send to you and know that it is
a reality. Many doubt the loving tasks that we do,
which keeps the energy from coming to its fullest
fruition. When doubt enters in, the energy of change
is not as strong, and then cannot be felt by those
that need it. When you ask, it is immediately sent
to you. If you have trouble feeling it, ask again. Ask
that it be given to you in a stronger, clearer way so
that you can truly sense it. Angels understand that
sometimes humans need to see to believe. Remember the story of Doubting Thomas in the Bible? The
Master Jesus understood this human tendency as
well, which is why he was able to teach to his dis-

ciple (and the rest of you in turn) this great lesson about believing without seeing. We are here, even if you cannot see us. Believe.

Educate yourself. Education is a strong antidote to fear. Many negative situations in the human world have improved through education. When people learn about the unknown, the power that the unknown has dissipates, and it is no longer feared. Learn all you can about any and all situations in your world, so that you can better combat fear and ignorance. Not every person will respond in a positive way when you try to enlighten him. The best way to help others to learn is to live by example. If you tell a person that what she believes is wrong, she may not respond positively to you because her life is still working on some level even though she is living in a negative way, or functioning from a place of fear. If you show her through your example how much better her life can be, then she may choose to move out of her negative pattern and into a more positive one. She will overcome her fear of the unknown, just as you have. Books bring people many positive things. Read and encourage others to seek their own information. Share what you know, and do not be afraid that you will not be accepted. Ask the angels to help you to integrate this knowledge to the world, and as you will, so it will be done.

Spiritual progression is possible for every soul. No one is exempt from this. Every person who has incarnated on the physical level is trying to learn and progress spiritually, even if he is not consciously aware of this choice. You cannot force anyone to recognize his own spiritual potential or even that he is here to grow. You can expose him to your own thoughts, feelings, and ideas, given and shared in love. What he chooses to do with this information is up to him.

For yourself, beloved: seek and you shall find. Knock and the door will be opened unto you. Sound familiar? There is some good information in that book, as well as in many other holy texts. Read it, study it, hold it in your heart and ask if it is truth. What feels right when examined from the heart and in the light of love is God's law. There are no other truths. You were made to discover these, and you have. And you will continue to discover them, and to live them throughout your Earthly existence.

Q.

In our lives, we face trials over and over again. Some of us seem to have many more hurdles than others. Some of us try as hard as we can to alleviate situations that make life seem unlivable or unmanageable. If we are in such a situation, or several of them back to back, where problems and obstacles seem to overwhelm us, how can we possibly achieve peace with ourselves and our life, with God and our guides, helpers, and spiritual matters? How can we be comfortable and grow to a point of understanding, acceptance, peace, and love so that we can go on and fulfill our mission here, and be in the best possible place mentally and spiritually?

A.

You ask here questions that are on the mind of every spiritually oriented human being, questions that seem to plague so many of you. Even asking this question says that you are in tune with your own spiritual nature, so congratulate yourself on your steady progression toward the Light that is God.

Remember, beloved child—you chose to incarnate at this time. When you made your choice, you were able to view the trials and challenges those in the Earth plane already faced before you were born, and yet you chose to come anyway. Again, you are to be congratulated for making this decision and being so committed to your own progression. As one human soul progresses, progression is made in the grander, bigger picture of the growth of all human kind. There is a larger evolution at work in the Universe as well, so every step forward, no matter how small it seems, is important and celebrated by Creator. Know this, and know that just as a parent cheers on her child, so God cheers you on as you continue the hard journey forward.

Your mental state is a choice, just as everything else in your life is a choice. Yes, it is easy to become entangled in the day-to-day stress and constant chaos that swirls around every human being. You cannot have a human experience without this. How you react to it, however, is an entirely different matter, and it is entirely up to you. Never doubt, though, that God and the angels are on your side and can help you to overcome all problems, no matter how great or small they are. How can you do this? I suggest beginning each day with prayer and meditation. Many will say, "Oh, I do not have time to do this." But you have time to eat breakfast in the morning or lunch in the afternoon. By eating, you nourish your body, which is essential to your survival. You must make prayer and meditation this important as well, for it is prayer and meditation that nourish your soul. How else can you feel connected to your Source? For this is what God is—the Source of All, the Source of Everything that is and Everything that is to be! You have unlimited access to this Source, and yet most of you ignore It. You do not spend even two minutes a day with It, when It is there for you at all times in limitless supply!

Do not mistake my tone. I do not reprimand you, beloved of God. I simply answer your question by pointing out to you all in a loving way how beneficial your connection to your Creator is. If you start your day by enveloping yourself in God's loving light and strengthen your connection to your Source, then the negative events and challenges of the day become minor inconveniences and small obstacles. They have no real meaning other than to remind you to do all that you do in love so that you can continue to perpetuate the feeling of peace and harmony you receive when sitting in God's loving presence.

There will always be obstacles, for every person chooses challenges before she comes into this lifetime, and sometimes creates more of them for herself as she journeys on. How she reacts to these obstacles is part of the growth process. It is all right to ask for help. It is all right to cry and to be upset, as long as you realize that tears are part of a cleansing and healing process that brings you back to a state of newness and beginnings. God has given you everything you need to overcome any challenges you face: intelligence, strength, faith, and His angels. Call on us for aid and guidance, and it is given to you. Ask that you recognize the guidance that is given to you when it comes, for it ALWAYS comes. And remember that no one is honored and blessed more than each of you for recognizing your own potential for spiritual growth and your willingness to undertake great challenges in coming into the physical body. You are growing and learning, and your attitude toward life is essential to how challenges present themselves in the future.

Q.

Where is mankind headed on this earth plane? It seems as though we have such little regard for human life as time moves on. I have stopped watching the local news reports (regardless of what region of the country I am in) because all they appear to cover are shootings, rapes, robberies, home invasions, and murders.

And why do people kill each other over religion? Of course, we all know that this has gone on for thousands of years. However, one would think that they might have come to some type of resolution by now.

A.

You highlight a question that is a source of frustration for many people who speak to God in their hearts and understand that love is the only answer that there is. However, just because you understand this does not mean that every soul understands. Remember that all actions are choices, and every human being has free will. Each action is a free will choice, even if it may not seem to be on the surface. At times, it may appear that circumstances force the hand of someone who makes a destructive choice, but this is not the case, because all souls have the ability to rise above fear and hate and choose love instead. All choices come from two feelings: fear or love. Which will you choose? In asking these related questions, it is obvious that you want to choose love, but there is still fear in your heart, as in the hearts of all humanity. And there are many negative circumstances in the human realm today that can stir fear. Many times, these fears are connected to the unknown, and so I tell you this: there is no unknown. All truth is in God. Seek God, and that connection to Him that is within you, and you shall never know fear.

The death and the disregard that you speak of in your question is a reaction to this fear. Many believe that disagreements over religion and belief can be quelled by dispatching the other side, the ones that do not agree with their views. Of course, you can see that this is foolish, but it is essential to understand in your compassion that this choice is one made from fear. Human beings fear what they do not understand. The choice is also often made because of ignorance. Do all you can to wipe out ignorance with education. In some parts of your society, people are raised from the time they are children to hate other cultures, other nations, other races. A child is NEVER born with hate in her heart. Hate is nurtured. It only grows when it is fed, and it feeds on fear and ignorance. Committing yourself to wiping these out is essential to rising above these attitudes.

In the angelic kingdoms, we understand that this task can be daunting to you. Hatred seems to be on the rise rather than becoming a thing of the past. But there will always be both love and hate, whether they are seen or unseen, because the Natural Law put in order by Creator dictates that there must be balance. You must always choose love over fear, however, if you wish to progress, and if you wish to bring spiritual growth to your world. Beloved, stop worrying about what other people are choosing and concentrate on what you yourself choose. Every moment is a choice to live in love or not to live in love. What are you choosing right now? It is not about being selfish. It is about focusing on your own choices and living what you believe, for this is the best way to educate others. When others see you living in love and not in fear, they will also see the peace and joy that radiates from you, for this is what is thus naturally attracted into your energy. They will then want this for themselves, and they will learn what they need to do in order to attract it. Be an example for others so that they, too, may learn.

It is not unwise to shield yourself from harmful and disturbing images, as you mention the news programs on television and the like. There is a difference in protecting yourself from these images, however, and burying your head in the sand, as humans like to say. You must still understand and recognize what goes on in the world around you, for this is how you can compassionately combat hate and violence. But you do not need to expose yourself to images and forms of communication that display anger, rage, murder, and other atrocities. Some humans use these as a form of entertainment. The angels do not understand this. We recognize the need for entertainment, and we understand the human need for expression in the form of music, film, art, and literature. However, a constant barrage of these disturbing elements only saturates your auric field with negative energy, thus making it harder to pull your energy back up into a loving, peaceful vibration. Think about this when you are choosing a movie to watch or a book to read. There are higher choices available that will benefit you and the rest of humanity in the long run.

Whether it is apparent or not, humankind does progress, and it is because of lightworkers like you that this progression continues. If you choose love over fear, then you are a lightworker, because you will bring light to others. This is the Light of God, and it is worth bearing. We honor you for doing this, and for incarnating during these troubling times. It is why I have chosen to reveal myself and my nature at this time, for humanity needs the help of the higher realms, and I AM available to all who seek me and my aid.

Q.

How can I develop a belief and faith in a Higher Power? How can one overcome the fear of death? How does one grieve over the loss of a loved one?

A.

Oh, beloved child of God, you ask about what many consider to be a complex thing, and yet faith is very simple. Faith simply is. How do you develop faith in science and the brilliant discoveries clever individuals have made over the many years of Earthly endeavors? You see these with your eyes, touch them with your hands, work with them every day, do you not? Many years ago, computers were not even a thought, and yet today, this answer is being typed on a computer. How wondrous your human ancestors would have thought this device to be! So it is with faith and God! You must work at developing a relationship with God to ever expect faith in God to exist.

How do you develop this relationship? How do you develop the relationships you have with others in your life? You talk to them, ask them questions and listen to their answers, interact with them as often as possible so that your relationship can stay fresh and alive. So it is with God! Can you not talk to God in prayer? Can you not speak to Him aloud or in your thoughts, asking Him questions, telling Him about your triumphs and your trials, praising Him for His goodness and His love? Can you not interact with God and His energy through prayer and ritual, whether it is in a church setting with others of a like mind or on your own, within your own private quarters?

I can hear what you might say: "But how do I know God is really there? I cannot see Him. I cannot touch Him or hear the answers He gives to my questions. I cannot believe in Him if I cannot have this type of contact with Him." Beloved, this is the essence of faith! You cannot expect to have a relationship with God if you are testing Him all the time. What if your friend invited you to dinner so that you could both relax and enjoy each other's company, and you said, "Well, I do not believe you are really my friend. In order for me to have dinner with you, you must prove your loyalty. Before I will go with you, you must stand on your head in traffic and then I will believe that you are indeed a true friend." What would your friend say? Would your friend not be terribly disappointed in your attitude? Would your friend not walk away from you, perhaps never call on you again? This is how it often is in human relationships. But God is ever-present, always loving, and will NEVER abandon you. You can test Him if you wish, by asking Him to bring something into your life to "prove" His existence, but if you are dwelling in a depressed or negative vibration, you may never recognize the gift that God definitely brings into your life. Ask, and you shall receive. But if you ask for a sports car and dwell in negativity, the Universe, which operates from the Mind of God, cannot possibly bring that to you, because you cannot attract positive things when you dwell in this mindset. But I caution you, too, beloved: God is not a game, to be taken out and toyed with on whims. God loves you, infinitely and beyond measure, and hopes that you will enter into a joyous relationship with Him. The easiest way to do this is to talk to Him. Open your heart to Him and allow His love to infuse your being. Understand that when you are in a joyful, loving energy, this is God at His most tangible and highest manifestation in the Earth plane. Appreciate the energy that He brings to you, when you sincerely seek Him and His ways!

You ask about grief and loss. I say to you truly: energy exists and sustains into infinity. All is energy. Every person is energy. Your scientists have said that energy can be neither created nor destroyed, and they are correct. And so you must understand that when a human being dies, the body that the soul inhabits falls away and decays, but the beautiful energy that is the Divine Essence lives on in another plane of existence. There are many planes, many worlds. I have spoken of these previously, and no, you may never encounter all of them during your physical incarnation. And yet they do exist, and so does the energy that was once your loved one. Knowing that this Divine energy never ends should help you to understand that the death of the physical body is not an ending but a beginning.

There is nothing to fear about these planes beyond the Earth, because all are infused with God's loving energy, and all are there to help every soul to further progression toward ultimate union with Creator.

Grief is a process unlike any other in the human experience. All human beings grieve, and it is natural to do so. When a loved one passes into the higher realms, her energy in the body will be missed by those left behind, and so humans grieve. But understanding that the loved one's soul essence carries on, moving ever toward God, should help those left in grief to move past sorrow and into a more joyful state. Union with God is a joyful event, and this should be celebrated. Human culture does not usually celebrate the death of someone because it is thought to be socially unacceptable to do so. However, this transition into pure spirit energy is a great cause for rejoicing in the other planes, because all of the souls that are a part of All That Is understand the great spiritual progression and love that the departed soul will feel in God's presence.

The angels understand and support you in your grief. Be gentle with yourself as you move through it; concentrate on the great gift your loved one has been given.

Q.

How do we reconcile all the contradictory statements in the different holy books? Are there holy writings that are more correct than others?

A.

Thank you for your excellent question. It is one that plagues many people, and one that is vital to an understanding of human spiritual progression.

Yes, there are many writings that are considered sacred or holy. The Torah, the Bible, the Quran, the Upanishads . . . all of these are important texts for the spiritual scholar to study. And they all, at times, present challenging information, and even principles that seem to contradict the other books. Why is this? Is it because Creator keeps changing His mind about His ways and His teachings?

I AM sure you find this idea humorous. Of course it is not because God is fallible. Humans are, and all of these writings have been filtered through the consciousness of individual people. Just as my thoughts are coming through the conduit who is writing this, so, too, did all of these sacred texts flow into the minds of human beings and thus onto paper or parchment so that others could read them.

Let us examine this process. A man is living at a certain time in history. All around him are troubles, challenges, issues that the man is trying to reconcile in his mind and heart. Perhaps these issues even bring a spiritual crisis to this man, and he turns to

God for answers. He prays to God that he be given insights into why such and so is happening at this time. God answers him, as God ALWAYS DOES, and the man feels compelled to sit down and write out the insights he has received concerning these challenges, these events, these issues. As he writes, God's message may be altered slightly, since the only way for God to get these teachings through is to use words that the man understands and can write down for others to understand as well. Does the man color what comes through from God? Perhaps, even if he is trying his best to bring through word for word what comes from Creator. Nevertheless, he eventually has an inspired document that he has written that has come from God.

Now, perhaps the man feels compelled to share this with his neighbors, because he knows that they are facing the same challenges and have the same questions about spiritual matters. Perhaps one of his neighbors is a foreigner in their land and speaks both his own language and the language of his native land. When he reads this message from God, he feels compelled to pass it on to his relatives and friends in his original country, for he knows they will benefit from the information received. He sits down and translates the writing into his own language so that others may read it. Does the message change slightly during the translation process? Yes, most likely, because different languages have different nuances of usage that cannot always be translated exactly. Still, the core meaning of the message remains, hopefully, so that others may benefit from God's wisdom.

But suppose as this message continues to make its way from community to community, there are some human beings who do not like the message. Perhaps for political or social reasons, the message does not resonate with their agenda, and they feel threatened by it. Could they possibly change the message themselves to reflect what they believe to be true? Of course. This has happened, too, in some cases, making some of the sacred writings false or flawed.

At other times, the sacred writings may have been reviewed by those in power, and certain writings were chosen over others to be the "true" and "best" writings. The men who chose these writings were, hopefully, doing their best to serve God at the time and trying to enlighten those who came to them for guidance by giving them the most accurate writings that came from Creator. Is there a way to be certain which writings are "better" and "most accurate"? That brings us to your other question.

What is truth to you? You can find truth when you bring yourself into a state of love and then examine a certain belief or writing. Think of something that brings you enormous pleasure, and feel the great joy you have when you experience this. Then sit with a piece of scripture that you question and see if the vibration of that scripture equals the same high vibration of joy. If it does not, then it does not resonate for you, and you should not follow it at this time. You must decide for yourself those writings that are "best." God will not pick and choose. God will, however, dedicate Himself to having a personal relationship with you. And this type of relationship can be even more beneficial than the study of all of the world's sacred writings, because it will be the most personal and the closest you can come to God during your physical incarnation.

Q.

Why do we, as humans, let ourselves be so easily swayed from one religion to another? Why don't the angels or Creator come down and say, "This is the true way?"

A.

Beloved, God will never tell you how to think, act, or feel, simply because so much of your spiritual progression relies on your ability to think, act, and feel freely! He has given to you, through human teachers, Master energies, sacred writings, and other signs guidelines for how to think, act, and feel, and yet the choice in these matters is always entirely up to you.

Remember, beloved: religion, the outward ritual and community of spirituality, is a human invention. Creator did not create religion. Humankind created religion because human souls like to cling together and find support for their beliefs and actions in others. There is nothing wrong with this, and this is not intended as a reprimand or a belittlement of the power of ritual, prayer, and other religious actions. However, it is important for souls to realize and understand why they migrate to a certain belief system or religion. Why do certain concepts resonate while others do not? The advanced spiritual soul is constantly questioning, constantly striving for comprehension, and constantly trying his best to work in love. While this may be seen by some as a swaying from one religious path to another, it is an important part of the progression process for some souls. As he tries on new ideas and concepts and participates in new rituals, the soul decides which exercises suit his energy best at this time in his life. Recall that not only is the soul evolving in a human being, but so is his intellect and his physical self. At certain ages, specific spiritual practices emphasized in certain religions may be more beneficial to the spiritual student than at other times. This is all part of progression! Do not be too judgmental when you notice a soul who does not seem comfortable in religious beliefs and always seems to be "trying on" new ideas. This is how some souls learn, and it is not for you to judge. Concern yourself only with your own progression, and know that there is room in God's house for all beliefs based in love.

Q.

If peace is a part of Natural Law, is not conflict a part of it as well, since peace is not the absence of conflict?

A.

It is good to continue to question the energy of peace within the Earth plane. Many human beings believe it is an unattainable state, and yet I say to you in truth: Nothing is impossible with God!

You are wise to see that there will always be both peace and conflict in the world. A part of Natural Law, as you point out, is the Law of Balance, which shows us that there cannot be one without the other. It is the degree to which conflict is present that can be modified. Is it not different to argue with your neighbor over where his fence is placed than to start a war over it? Is it not within the realm of possibility to find a peaceful solution to this conflict? I tell you, it is ALWAYS within the realm of possibility to find the peaceful solution to ANY conflict.

I hear what some of you might say: "Ah, Metatron. What about the wars? What about the conflicts of religion, of ideology, that plague our world today?" And I say to you in truth: these conflicts are man-made, NOT God-made. God welcomes dialogue, debate, and even conflict between the many religions, the many ideologies, because this is how all grow spiritually and come to understandings about respect, love, sharing, compassion, and other virtues that God cherishes. God does NOT welcome war that lays waste to the lands of the Earth and sacrifices the precious lives of his beloved creations. The challenge in these instances is not to overcome conflict. Conflict will always be present. The challenge is in HOW the conflict is overcome. Is the conflict resolved through negotiations, through intelligent reasoning, and through loving compromise? Or is the conflict resolved through violence? Unfortunately, many times, humanity chooses the easiest path, which is to resolve the conflict through violence, not realizing that when the conflict is resolved this way, it only leads to MORE CONFLICT in the future.

Each person must reflect on conflict in his or her individual life and find ways to overcome conflict through peaceful resolution. Many great souls who have been on the Earth plane have taught how to do this through their example. These lessons must be taught to children, so that they can further the peace vibration and bring loving resolution to conflicts, large and small, in their own lives and experiences. The issue is not to wipe out conflict but rather to approach and resolve it from a place of love. This keeps the Law of Balance in harmony within the Universe and still achieves the ultimate goal of peace throughout the Earth.

Q.

Please comment on the workings of the cosmos—Natural Law. I feel certain that there are many principles that haven't been discovered, or that have been known in the past but then lost. Can we work productively with Natural Law if we don't know the law with which we are working?

A.

It is good that you ask for more information about Natural Law, for it is these Universal Laws upon which All That Is exists. I will tell you, beloved child: all the knowledge of Natural Law that has always existed still exists and has been revealed to humanity through sacred writings, through ritual, through channels such as this one with whom I work—it is always in motion, for it can never be forsaken or ignored. Such is the working of the Universe and all the worlds that Creator has made. Human understanding of Natural Law, however, is flawed in some ways, simply because of the nature of human existence. Yes, the spiritual pilgrim may recognize her own connection to Divinity and thus live in accordance with that Divine energy, and yet she may never fully understand that all knowledge of All That Is is ever-present and ever-accessible to her. Why? Because her mind is human, and often it is the mind of a person that keeps her from accessing her connection to Divinity and her communion with God. Doubt, fear, shame, guilt—these human feelings keep her sometimes from pursuing this connection.

If she were in a constant communion with Divinity, she would no longer be in the body and thus would exist only as energy in one of the many planes of existence that seeks to meld with Creator. As she is in the body, she strives forward on her spiritual progression, and part of that is trying to understand Natural Law. Will she ever succeed in this understanding? Perhaps. There have been Masters before on the Earth plane that have achieved this. Jesus the Christ. Buddha. Saint Germain. These may be names you recognize, and it would do well for you to study their teachings and to see how Natural Law applies in their lives, for then you may well see how their understandings brought them to deeper, more spiritual existences and thus moved them further on their spiritual journeys and closer to God.

Put simply: the greatest Natural Law is the Law of Love. No other Natural Law can function without this one. The Master Jesus summed this up in his teaching, and it is this pure state to which all humanity must aspire. When a person dwells in the vibration of pure, unadulterated love, she cannot help but act in accordance with all of the other Natural Laws of the Universe. By being in a state of perfect love, she thus creates around herself the vibration of love, which draws to her, through the Law of Attraction, the circumstances, people, and events that she needs to continuously sustain this energy. This is, indeed, the Law of Vibration. You can start to see here how all of the Natural Laws begin to fall into place, like a telescope opened up to view the stars. All of the Laws fold back in upon themselves, coming back to the beginning, the Law of Love. There is no greater Law, no greater aspiration as spiritual beings, and no other Law to worry about in the grand sense of spiritual knowledge.

However, many people have a difficult time dwelling in love on a constant basis. Why? Because they have not been taught the great importance of this. It is also because they do not understand what dwelling in love actually feels like. It is a transcendent feeling that takes a person beyond cares for self, cares for earthly goods, and cares for earthly concerns. If you were to maintain this state of pure love, your vibration would rise so high that you would ascend to the other worlds, much like Jesus did. So much is possible, and yet so many people choose to dwell in thoughts of lack, unhappiness, anger, resentment . . . the list is endless.

If you are choosing love and doing your best to work within the love vibration, then you are working in accordance with Natural Law, and all of the other Natural Laws will fall into place. Study them if you wish, for they are interesting unto themselves, but a deep understanding of them is not necessary for your own Divine progression.

Q.

Do you have suggestions for manifesting desires? How can we best get to that "feeling place" that increases our attraction with what we desire?

A.

It is good that you ask about the Law of Attraction, beloved child, for God wants all of His creations to be happy and fulfilled during their lifetimes. The Natural Law of Attraction has been operating since the beginning of time, given to humanity as a way of manifesting true happiness and eliminating want, and yet many do not understand it or how it works.

You understand already, beloved, that you must FEEL happy to ATTRACT more happiness in your life, whether the happiness comes in the form of material things, people, events, experiences, etc. It is not selfish or egotistical to want possessions and experiences. There is no lack in the world; this is flawed, human thinking. The Law of Abundance, another Natural Law, states that all is available to everyone at all times, and there is no limited source. The Source of All is completely unlimited! To think that someone would consider God, the Source, to be limited in any way! Do you see the flaw in this thought? Therefore, since there is no lack, anything and everything can be yours, but you must first be in a vibration of happiness in order to attract it.

There are many exercises that will help you to become happier and more centered on joy. Gratitude is one feeling you should practice routinely, for when you are grateful for what you already have, you build joy within yourself, and thus you attract more and more joy to your energy field. Write down every day something for which you are grateful. Write down many things! If you are having trouble in a relationship, write down the things about that person for which you are grateful. Focus on these attributes instead of the qualities you dislike. Say out loud, "I am grateful for . . ." This gives even more energy to the process and builds the happiness vibration even higher. This is the easiest and best way to constantly stay in the energy of happiness that will help you to attract the events and possessions you wish to have in your life.

Q.

I understand the concept of living in the moment and trusting that we are exactly where we need to be (everything for a reason). What I don't understand, and could really use help with now, is how we know we're on the right life path. I'm not talking spiritually; I'm referring to whatever it is we're supposed to be doing or would be good at doing while we're here—our earthly profession, so to speak: teacher, garbageman, stay-at-home mom, and so on.

Q.

We are told to follow our bliss. What is the best way to determine what our bliss is? Is this different than our purpose to being here on earth?

A.

I asked the one with whom I work to put these two questions together so I can comment on both, for the answer to the first lies within the second. You ask about purpose and about bliss. Do you not understand yet, beloved child of God, that you came into this lifetime to live in bliss? What is bliss but a feeling of unlimited and unadulterated joy? This feeling is what it means to be one with God. This feeling is what is experienced in the higher realms on a constant basis. In the lifetime that you have chosen, you have asked to progress spiritually by encountering hardships, challenges, lessons. When you encounter these, you should praise God, for it is in overcoming them that you achieve your spiritual progression! But it is uplifting yourself to a state of joyful living that helps you to understand, appreciate, and accept your connection to God. You can NEVER sever this connection, no matter what you do. It will always be there, and it is this connection and your experience of it that brings to you this blissful state. It is this state that God wishes for you, in every moment of every day. Is it impossible for you to attain this bliss as you are living in the human world, with all of its upheavals? Nothing is impossible, I tell you truly, for even in the worst of circumstances, the glimmers of hope, love, and happiness that you see can elevate you back to your blissful state. Is this difficult? It does not need to be. I have spoken to you about choosing love over fear. Within this choice always lies the blissful state of being that you seek. When you choose love, you shall always move closer to bliss. You cannot move away from it if your choice is truly infused with love.

How do you recognize bliss? Think for a moment of times in your life when you have felt the happiest, the most peaceful, the most joyful. You have these moments—you do, no matter what your circumstances or challenges. Realize that these moments are ways for you to recognize the blissful state, and sit silently in this feeling as you relive that experience. How do you feel? What does bliss feel like? Where is it in your body? Let its energy infuse your being.

Ask me to help you to remember what this feels like when you need a reminder. All of the angels can aid you in recognizing this and reaching this feeling. Can you live like this every moment of every day? Of course. I hear you say in your mind, "Ah, Metatron, that is wishful thinking." Yes, it is wishful thinking, and this is the thinking that you need to maintain! God wants to hear your wishes, your dreams, your hopes. Is not living in bliss, in absolute happiness, one of those? All is possible with God! How can we angels help you achieve these states if you do not aspire to them? Ask, ask, ask! We await your call.

Now that you understand bliss, live in it, in every way possible. This includes your work on the Earth plane. Why do you stay in unhappy circumstances? Do you expect others to make you happy? This is a flawed expectation, for no one in your life can make you happy except yourself. You know this intellectually—I tell you nothing you do not already understand. And yet you stay in an unfulfilling job or an unloving relationship because you think or hope it will get better. You cannot control anyone else's choices but your own. If someone chooses to be unhappy, you cannot force him or even coerce him into bliss. This is something he must recognize and choose for himself. But this does not mean that you must stay with him in this unhappy state.

Look at your life. In what moments are you most happy, closest to God and to your own state of bliss? Is it when you work with your children or play games with them? Perhaps you need to work with other children outside your home, as a teacher or caregiver. Are you happiest when you are with your pets? Maybe your bliss lies in caring for animals in some capacity. Do you enjoy talking with your friends? Perhaps a blissful career can be found for you in teaching adults, in counseling, or in customer service. Each of you has been given unique talents by Creator. Take time to recognize what these are, and then serve yourself by serving your talents. When you feel most happy, this is your bliss, and this is what you should focus on as your work and your life. For some, it will mean going back to school to earn degrees necessary in your society. So be it. Trust that the angels will bring to you the resources that you need to achieve your ends. We will be happy to help you . . . which brings us closer to God and to our bliss.

Q.

How can we help people realize their true potential in this
life and then aid them in going forward with it? And how
can we better spread the word about the angels, helping
others understand that this work is of God and not of evil?
Can you give us information on how to proceed with this
project?

Q.

What should I be doing to help others?

A.

Beloved Light of God, how wonderful that you think
of others and how you can serve them! This is in itself
a noble calling, and one that helps you to evolve and
progress spiritually as you strive to achieve these
higher vibrations that love and service bring. We
angels are speaking to many of you, whispering our
messages and trying to intercede in order to make
Creator's bright, inspiring message accessible to all.
Those of you who are lightworkers feel the urge, the
pull, to be of service to others, and you step forward
out of the darkness of fear and into the Light of Love
so that you can spread the Good News to those who
need to hear it. Whether they accept it or reject it is
not the issue, nor is it your responsibility and duty to
convince them. Your only mission is to stand in your
truth and proclaim it. Some will do this through quiet,
unnoticed service to others. Some will do it in a more
public way, perhaps by writing a book, or by teach-

ing a class, or by performing healing, or through ritual or prayer. The method by which you convey this loving vibration to others will be revealed to you by how you feel in performing these tasks. You will feel uplifted and inspired; you will feel close to All That Is, and this will raise your own spiritual vibration to a higher frequency, allowing more goodness, light, and love to come into your life. This will feed the cycle of energy that will allow you to do more and better work. It does not matter how the work is done, for each individual must embrace God's message and put it into practice in his own personal life. And yet those of you who do serve others are to be commended, not because you are "better," but because you recognize the need for the message to be passed on.

The angels are constant bridges between humanity and God, and we work incessantly to modify the vibration of love and to make it more real and more vital to human souls. Sometimes it is very difficult for a human soul to feel God's loving presence. These souls feel trapped in darkness, yet there is always light, and the knowledge that it is within each soul is a fact that we Messengers try our best to impart. We work with these souls to impress upon their minds and hearts in ways that they can understand and accept that goodness and light do surround them, whether they choose to see them or not. Sometimes, we are able to send human messengers to these souls so that they can bring this communication to them in a more tangible way. This is you, beloved of God; this is your role as a lightworker, in whatever capacity you fulfill it. Sometimes just your presence is enough to help another soul. Sometimes your skills are utilized to bring peace, healing, or comfort. Sometimes a simple smile that you impart to another is the one blessing that brings her out of darkness and into light! Never underestimate what a large impact small actions may have, and endeavor to continue to bring your love, which is a reflection of Creator's Divine love, to all people and situations in your life.

Ignorance is a by-product of fear. People fear what they do not understand, as I have mentioned in our previous communications. Some fear the idea of angels because we are supposedly supernatural, that is, not of the natural world. And yet I say to you in truth: God created angels just as He created humanity, and He charged us with assisting the human race in every way we can. We take our commission very seriously and rejoice in the opportunity to serve afforded to us in this duty. When some human souls reject us as figments of imagination or as something evil, we do not condemn them, for we understand that this is a part of their own spiritual progression. It may seem to some that this would not be progression but regression, but it is not. It simply is, and we respect every point that any soul reaches in their spiritual learning, whether it includes us or not. At least when a person rejects the kingdom of angels, he is actually considering his place in the Universe and how he connects with Creator. Should you try to convince this person that we exist, or that he should rethink his position? You can simply offer him, in the humblest way, your own experience and allow him to make his own decision. When you bring a light to someone, he can choose to put it on the table and illuminate the whole room, or he can choose to blow it out and remain in darkness. What he chooses is not your responsibility.

The angels are pleased to work with any lightworker who seeks with true sincerity to raise the vibration of the Universe by speaking and enacting God's great message of love. Ask us to be with you to assist in this process. We will help you by manipulating energies in your environment to be more conducive to the spreading of this message, and by impressing upon you ways to make the message easier to impart. Sit with us in meditation; write with us as this one does with whom I work; pray with us to create a more loving, compassionate Universe. What you see in your mind, you can create within your world. This is a Natural Law, and I tell you in truth: it is so. You can create it from your highest intention, and we can lend our energies to your creation.

————

As you can see from this chapter, Metatron is willing and able to answer any questions posed to him, as long as they are asked lovingly and with deep respect. Do you have an issue you would like Metatron to address or a situation upon which you would welcome some angelic insight? Practice the inspirational writing techniques given in this section and see what Metatron reveals to you.

Endings and Beginnings

Today, as I finish writing this book, the first day of spring has arrived in my part of the world. The sun shines through the double glass doors in my dining room. My dachshund has hopped up onto the ottoman in the living room, barking for all he's worth as my next-door neighbor washes his car in the driveway. Earlier today, as I walked my dog through the neighborhood, I noticed tiny purple flowers pushing through the soil at the street corner, and the pointed heads of yellow daffodils ripening on their stems. The cool air sifting through my screened window is ripe with change, the blessing that every spring season brings to all of us.

No matter what time of year it is as you read this, change is waiting inside of you, too. Like a dormant seed in springtime, it is ready to rise, then burst open as a beautiful, fragrant flower.

Throughout this book, you have learned exercises and ideas for communicating with the Archangel Metatron to benefit your spiritual growth and progress toward enlightenment. What you do with this information now is entirely up to you. Recognize, however, that positive change is always within your power, and Metatron, like all the angels, is just an invocation away.

I have enjoyed the time we've spent together in these pages, and the discoveries I have made about myself and my world while working with Metatron on this book. It is my full and loving intention to continue communicating with the Archangel, for I have seen the power and scope of his intercession. His loving presence in my life has brought me a balance and peace that I've not known before. I hope that you will join us in working toward the same ends for yourself, and for the betterment of our entire human family.

Until we meet again, loving seeker and worker in the Light, I wish you blessings, peace, and joy. Thank you for allowing me to serve.

$\mathcal{B}$ibliography

Books

Cabot, Laurie. *A Salem Witch's Herbal Magic* (Salem, MA: Celtic Crow Publishing, 1994).

Cabot, Laurie, with Tom Cowan. *Power of the Witch* (New York: Delta Publishing, 1989).

Dennis, Rabbi Geoffrey W. *The Encyclopedia of Jewish Myth, Magic, and Mysticism* (Woodbury, MN: Llewellyn Publications, 2007).

Hopking, C. J. M. *The Practical Kabbalah Guidebook* (New York: Sterling Publishing Company, 2001).

Howitt, William. *The History of the Supernatural in All Ages and Nations, and in All Churches, Christian and Pagan: Demonstrating a Universal Faith* (Ann Arbor: University of Michigan Library, 2005). First published 1863 by J.P. Lippincott & Co., Philadelphia.

Melody. *Love Is in the Earth: A Kaleidoscope of Crystals* (Wheatridge, CO: Earth-Love Publishing House, 1991).

Pollack, Rachel. *The Kabbalah Tree: A Journey of Balance and Growth* (St. Paul, MN: Llewellyn Publications, 2004).

RavenWolf, Silver. *Angels: Companions in Magick* (St. Paul, MN: Llewellyn Publications, 1996).

———. *To Ride a Silver Broomstick: New Generation Witchcraft* (St. Paul, MN: Llewellyn Publications, 1993).

Stewart, R. J. *The Miracle Tree: Demystifying the Qabalah* (Franklin Lakes, NJ: The Career Press, 2003).

Stone, Michael E., and Theodore A. Bergren, eds. 1998. *Biblical Figures Outside the Bible* (Harrisburg, PA: Trinity Press, 1998). "From Son of Adam to Second God: Transformations of the Biblical Enoch," by Philip S. Alexander.

Three Initiates. *The Kybalion: A Study of the Hermetic Philosophy of Ancient Egypt and Greece* (Chicago: Yogi Publication Society, 1908).

Tyson, Donald. *Enochian Magic for Beginners* (St. Paul, MN: Llewellyn Publications, 1997).

Vanden Eynden, Rose. *So You Want to Be a Medium? A Down-to-Earth Guide* (Woodbury, MN: Llewellyn Publications, 2006).

Virtue, Doreen. *Archangels and Ascended Masters: A Guide to Working and Healing with Divinities and Deities* (Carlsbad, CA: Hay House, 2003).

———. *Healing with the Angels* (Carlsbad, CA: Hay House, 1999).

Williams-Heller, Anne. *Kabbalah: Your Path to Inner Freedom* (Wheaton, IL: The Theosophical Publishing House/ Quest Books, 1990).

Internet Resources

168 Feng Shui Advisors, "Yin and Yang Theory," www.168fengshui.com/blog/2005/08/05/yin-and -yang-theory.

Crystalinks, Ellie Crystal's Metaphysical and Science Website, "Metatron" at www.crystalinks.com/ metatron.html and "Enoch" at www.crystalinks.com/ enoch.html.

LightSource Arts, "An Introduction to Sacred Geometry," www.sacred-geometry.com/bruce-rawles_sacred _geometry.html.

San Graal Library, www.sangraal.com/library/dedicated .htm.

Sananda's Eagles, "Metatron," www.sanandaseagles.com/ gai/pages/metatron.html.

Index

To Write to the Author

If you wish to contact the author or would like more information about this book, please write to the author in care of Llewellyn Worldwide and we will forward your request. Both the author and publisher appreciate hearing from you and learning of your enjoyment of this book and how it has helped you. Llewellyn Worldwide cannot guarantee that every letter written to the author can be answered, but all will be forwarded. Please write to:

Rose Vanden Eynden
℅ Llewellyn Worldwide
2143 Wooddale Drive, Dept. 978-0-7387-1343-4
Woodbury, MN 55125-2989, U.S.A.

Please enclose a self-addressed stamped envelope for reply,
or $1.00 to cover costs. If outside U.S.A., enclose
international postal reply coupon.

Many of Llewellyn's authors have websites with additional information and resources. For more information, please visit our website at:

www.llewellyn.com